Sean Ell is an experienced barrister specialising in immigration, asylum and nationality law. Prior to practising at the Bar of England and Wales, he was accredited by the Law Society as an immigration and asylum specialist from 2005 and as a supervisor from 2006. He took on a supervisory role at a national charity providing immigration advice, before moving on to work as the immigration supervisor at a Law Centre and then at a regional firm of solicitors.

Sean is ranked as a Leading Junior in immigration law in the Legal 500 (Tier 2 – 2023 edition). He was appointed by the Medical Practitioners Tribunal as a Tribunal member in 2011, as a Tribunal Chair in 2015 and as a Legally Qualified Chair in 2019.

A Practical Guide to Deprivation of British Citizenship

A Practical Guide to Deprivation of British Citizenship

Sean Ell

Barrister, Inner Temple

LLB (Hons)

Law Brief Publishing

Published 2023 by Law Brief Publishing, an imprint of Law Brief Publishing Ltd
30 The Parks
Minehead
Somerset
TA24 8BT

www.lawbriefpublishing.com

Paperback: 978-1-913715-06-9

Dedicated to all those who have helped and encouraged me throughout my career especially my wife.

PREFACE

For a number of years, consecutive Secretaries of State for the Home Department have increasingly used their powers to deprive individuals of their British citizenship. The use of those powers was recently brought to the public's attention through the widespread publicity of the case of Shamima Begum and the political debate arising out of section 10 of the Nationality and Borders Act 2022, which provides the power to deprive without giving notice.

With the continued growth of decisions to deprive individuals of their British citizenship, the acquisition of British citizenship is no longer the conclusive end to people's immigration journey that it once was. Further, those born British citizens are no longer guaranteed to continue to hold it until their death. The need to successfully challenge deprivation decisions is therefore becoming increasingly commonplace for practitioners.

This book aims to provide a practical guide to assist practitioners in the evolving area of deprivation of British citizenship, exploring the ways and process by which an individual could lose their British citizenship, as well as the consequences for them, and potentially their family. It also covers the available options and approaches to challenging decisions in light of a number of recent and important judgments including **Begum** and **Chimi (deprivation appeals; scope and evidence) Cameroon [2023] UKUT 00115 (IAC)**.

The law is correct as of 31 May 2023.

Sean Ell
June 2023

CONTENTS

CHAPTER ONE

DEPRIVATION OF CITIZENSHIP

It has been possible in the UK to remove an individual's citizenship since the British Nationality and Status of Aliens Act 1914. Various changes over the past one hundred years have been made by Parliament to alter and amend the circumstances in which the power to deprive an individual of their citizenship can be exercised.

However, it is only since 2003 that individuals who have British citizenship other than by naturalisation can be deprived of their citizenship. The Nationality, Immigration and Asylum Act 2002 allowed for British born nationals who also hold another nationality to be deprived of their British citizenship, if they had done something '*seriously prejudicial*' to the UK's vital interests. This has subsequently been changed to when it is '*conducive to the public good*'. Such language affords the Secretary of State a great deal of latitude as to when the discretionary power to deprive an individual might be utilised.

Recent changes included in the Nationality and Borders Act 2022 show how the law continues to evolve, with the focus on broadening the circumstances in which the Secretary of State's power can be exercised.

Historically, only a small number of orders depriving individuals of their citizenship have been made. From 2010 to 2018, on average 19 people a year were deprived of their citizenship where it was conducive to the public good. In the same period on average 17 people a year were deprived of citizenship on the ground of fraud. Between 2010 to 2021 Home Office data shows at least 767 citizenship deprivation orders were made, of which at least 550 have been made on fraud grounds, and 217 orders for the '*public good*'[1].

Although the data is limited, it seemingly supports the anecdotal evidence that numbers are increasing, as seen by the growing number of appeals being heard in the Tribunal which was almost 1200 between 1 April 2015 and 30 September 2022[2]. Recent high-profile cases such as Shamima Begum and the Rochdale groomers show the political desire in pursuing deprivation orders, as such it appears deprivation will be an area of immigration work that will continue to grow.

1 Deprivation of British citizenship and withdrawal of passports, House of Common Library, Research Briefing 25 January 2023

2 Tribunal Statistics Quarterly: July to September 2022, Published 8 December 2022

CHAPTER TWO

BRITISH NATIONALITY LAW OVERVIEW

Nationality can be a complex area of law. Historical changes from an Empire to the Commonwealth have seen a number of measures, often for political reasons, taken to create different categories of British nationality and to limit those who are British.

There are currently six different types of British nationality:

i) British citizenship

ii) British Overseas Territories citizen (known as British dependent territories citizenship before 26 February 2002)

iii) British overseas citizenship

iv) British subject

v) British national (overseas)

vi) British protected person

This book examines how individuals with the most common type of British nationality, British citizenship, can be deprived of it.

British citizenship

British citizenship is by far the most common type of British nationality.

The main legislation governing British citizenship is the British Nationality Act 1981 'BNA 1981'. Whether an individual is a British citizen, rather than one of the other categories is important. As a British citizen an individual has the right of abode in the United Kingdom 'UK' (s.2 of the Immigration Act 1971). Those with the right of abode "*shall be free to live in, and to come and go into and from, the United Kingdom without let or hindrance*" subject to restrictions to enable that right to be established e.g., production of a valid British passport.

An individual will usually become a British citizen by either:

i) Automatic acquisition

ii) Naturalisation

iii) Registration

The manner by which an individual acquired their British citizenship can be relevant to the question of whether and in what circumstances they can be deprived of their citizenship. It is therefore important to know how it is that the individual became a British citizen when dealing with cases where deprivation is a real possibility.

CHAPTER THREE

DEPRIVATION LAW AND GUIDANCE

The Secretary of State's power to deprive an individual of their British citizenship is set out in the British Nationality Act 1981 'the BNA 1981'.

The BNA 1981 was brought in to update the laws relating to British nationality, which had been significantly amended since the previous British Nationality Act 1948 had come into force. The BNA 1981 has itself seen significant changes since it came into force, with the latest changes being made by the Nationality and Borders Act 2022. Section 10 of the Nationality and Borders Act 2022 makes a number of important changes to the BNA 1981 with regard to notification of deprivation. Not all of the changes made by the Nationality and Borders Act 2022 to the BNA 1981 have come into force yet.

Changes to legislation

The BNA 1981 has been in force since 1 January 1983. For 20 years after that, the BNA 1981 remained consistent in that that the Secretary of State could by order deprive an individual their citizenship if they had acquired their citizenship by registration or naturalisation, if satisfied that:

(i) The registration or naturalisation had been obtained by fraud, false representation or concealment of material fact: s40(1);

(ii) the individual had shown disloyalty of disaffection towards Her Majesty by act or speech: s40(3)(a);

(iii) the person had unlawfully traded or communicated with an enemy during any war in which Her Majesty was engaged or been engaged in or associated with any business carried out to assist an enemy in that war: s40(3)(b); or

(iv) the person had been sentenced in any country to twelve months or more imprisonment within five years of the date of naturalisation or registration and the person would not become stateless: s40(3)(c), s40(5)(b).

Deprivation could take place in each case only if the Secretary of State was satisfied that it was not conducive to the public good that the individual should continue to be a British citizen.

The Nationality Immigration and Asylum Act 2002 came into force on 1 April 2003. It amended the BNA 1981 in three significant respects by introducing a general power to deprive a person of citizenship status if satisfied that the person had done anything "seriously prejudicial to the vital interests of the UK or a British overseas territory". That "seriously prejudicial" power was not to be used if the Secretary of State was satisfied that to do so would make a person stateless (s.40(4) as was). Finally, the Act extended the power to include individuals whose citizenship was acquired by birth.

With effect from 16 June 2006, the "seriously prejudicial" requirement was replaced by the lower hurdle that the Secretary of State need only be satisfied that "deprivation is conducive to the public good".

Current Statutory Powers: Section 40 of the BNA 1981

Section 40 of the BNA 1981 sets out the power to deprive individuals of their British nationality, with s.40(1) making clear that the power to deprive an individual of their "*citizenship status*" includes whether the individual status is as a British citizen, a British Overseas Territories citizen, a British Overseas citizen, a British National (Overseas), a British protected person, or as a British subject.

Section 40 provides for two circumstances in which an individual may be deprived of their British nationality:

(i) Where the Secretary of State considers it is conducive to the public good (s.40(2)); and

(ii) Where registration or naturalisation has been obtained by way of fraud, false representation, or concealment of a material fact (s.40(3))

In **Pirzada (Deprivation of citizenship: general principles)**[3] the Upper Tribunal held that:

> *"The separation of sub-ss (2) and (3) makes it clear that obtaining naturalisation by one of the means of deception set out in sub-s (3) cannot of itself amount to a reason enabling the Secretary of State to be satisfied that deprivation is conducive to the public good for the purposes of sub-s (2); but, in an appropriate case, there would appear to be no reason why the Secretary of State should not be satisfied that the conditions under both subsections exist."*

Current Statutory Powers: Section 40A of the BNA 1981

Section 40A of the BNA 1981 sets out the right of appeal that an individual might have against a decision made in respect of the under section 40 of the BNA 1981. That appeal will be either to the First-Tier Tribunal (IAC) or to SIAC, depending on the circumstances of the decision to deprive.

[3] [2017] UKUT 196 (IAC)

Current Statutory Powers: Section 40B of the BNA 1981

Section 40B of the BNA provides for the requirement by the Secretary of State to review the power given under section 40(4A). Section 40(4A) states:

> *"S.40(4A) But that does not prevent the Secretary of State from making an order under subsection (2) to deprive a person of a citizenship status if—*
>
> *(a) the citizenship status results from the person's naturalisation,*
>
> *(b) the Secretary of State is satisfied that the deprivation is conducive to the public good because the person, while having that citizenship status, has conducted him or herself in a manner which is seriously prejudicial to the vital interests of the United Kingdom, any of the Islands, or any British overseas territory, and*
>
> *(c) the Secretary of State has reasonable grounds for believing that the person is able, under the law of a country or territory outside the United Kingdom, to become a national of such a country or territory"*

Section 40(4A) was inserted by the Immigration Act 2014, and conferred upon the Secretary of State the power to deprive a person of British citizenship resulting from naturalisation, in circumstances where the consequence of that order is to render the person stateless. The power maybe exercised in circumstances where both s.40(4A)(b) and (c) apply. It was brought in following the failed attempt to deprive Hilal al-Jedda, a naturalised British citizen, of his citizenship. The law as it had stood since April 2003, meant there could be no deprivation of citizenship when the Secretary of State was satisfied that this would render a person stateless. Despite seeking to argue that Mr al-Jedda's Iraqi citizenship had revived or alternatively that he had made himself stateless by failing to apply for Iraqi Citizenship, the Supreme Court disagreed with the Secretary of State (in **Secretary of State for Home Department v Al-Jedda[4]).**

During its passage through the parliamentary process, the power to render an individual stateless was considered sufficiently controversial, having few international parallels, that a statutory provision for a review of the power to be inserted into the BNA 1981. The requirements for the Secretary of State to conduct a review as required by section 40B are that:

> *"(1) The Secretary of State must arrange for a review of the operation of the relevant deprivation power to be carried out in relation to each of the following periods—*
>
> *(a) the initial one year period;*
>
> *(b) each subsequent three year period.*
>
> *(2) The "relevant deprivation power" is the power to make orders under section 40(2) to deprive persons of a citizenship status in the circumstances set out in section 40(4A).*
>
> *(3) A review must be completed as soon as practicable after the end of the period to which the review relates.*
>
> *(4) As soon as practicable after a person has carried out a review in relation to a particular period, the person must—*
>
> *(a) produce a report of the outcome of the review, and*
>
> *(b) send a copy of the report to the Secretary of State.*
>
> *(5) The Secretary of State must lay before each House of Parliament a copy of each report sent under subsection (4)(b).*

4 [2013] UKSC 62, 9 October 20130

(6) The Secretary of State may, after consultation with the person who produced the report, exclude a part of the report from the copy laid before Parliament if the Secretary of State is of the opinion that it would be contrary to the public interest or prejudicial to national security for that part of the report to be made public.

(7) The Secretary of State may—

(a) make such payments as the Secretary of State thinks appropriate in connection with the carrying out of a review, and

(b) make such other arrangements as the Secretary of State thinks appropriate in connection with the carrying out of a review (including arrangements for the provision of staff, other resources and facilities).

(8) In this section—

"initial one year period" means the period of one year beginning with the day when section 40(4A) comes into force;

"subsequent three year period" means a period of three years beginning with the first day after the most recent of—

(a) the initial one year period, or

(b) the most recent subsequent three year period."

The first report was published by the Independent Reviewer, David Anderson QC in April 2016. The report covered the period from 30 July 2014 to 29 July 2015. The report noted that as of the date of publication there had been no exercise of the power at the time the report had gone to print. In providing a helpful review of the evolution of the power the report noted that neither of the two principal international Conventions which seek to avoid incidents of statelessness (1961 UN Convention on the Reduction of Statelessness & Council of Europe 1997 European

Convention on Nationality) prevent the UK from exercising the power under s.40(4A).

The report noted that the statute affords the Secretary of State a breadth of discretion. The use of the power is not contingent on an individual receiving a conviction for a terrorist offence but only on the deprivation being conducive to the public good because the individual, has conducted him or herself in a manner which is seriously prejudicial to the vital interests of the United Kingdom.

The report addressed a number of specific reservations about the power, some of which were raised by the Human Rights (Joint Select Committee) 'JCHR' and which may however, in the event the Secretary of State exercised the power, be in issue in future legal challenges. The observations included: –

(i) The Government's refusal to accept the applicability of the ECHR to out of-country deprivations;

(ii) The absence of a specific statutory requirement that the best interests of any children are treated as a primary consideration;

(iii) Differential treatment of natural-born and naturalised citizens;

(iv) The absence of a specific statutory requirement that "a proportionality approach" will be adopted by the Secretary of State.

(v) The "retrospective nature of the power", as the JCHR described it, by which is meant its application to persons who already have British citizenship by naturalisation;

(vi) The absence of a legal requirement that, in challenging the deprivation of citizenship in the Special Immigration

Appeals Commission, the individual must be shown the gist of the case against him, sufficient to enable him to instruct counsel (the so-called AF disclosure obligation);

(vii) The application of the residence test for legal aid to appeals to the First-Tier Tribunal, and the calculation of time limits for appeal;"

Secretary of State's Guidance

The Home Office has issued separate and updated caseworker guidance on deprivation[5] and nullity cases on 10 May 2023. This replaced the previous version which dated back to 27 July 2017, and covered both deprivation and nullity. The previous guidance reflected the old Chapter 55 guidance and had been in modernisation for a significant period of time.

---

5 'Deprivation of British citizenship', Version 1.0, 10 May 2023

CHAPTER FOUR

SECTION 40(2) – 'CONDUCIVE TO THE PUBLIC GOOD'

Section 40(2) of the British Nationality Act 1981 'the BNA 1981' provides that:

> *"The Secretary of State may by order deprive a person of a citizenship status if the Secretary of State is satisfied that deprivation is conducive to the public good."*

The decision to deprive a person of British citizenship under section 40(2) is taken in the exercise of a discretionary power on the basis of the Secretary of State's assessment of the public interest in an individual's case.

Section 40(4) of the BNA 1981 provides, however, that the Secretary of State may not make such an order "*if he is satisfied that the order would make a person stateless*". Section 40(4A) adds the following caveats to the limitation in section 40(4):

> *"(4A) But that does not prevent the Secretary of State from making an order under subsection (2) to deprive a person of a citizenship status if—*
>
> *(a) the citizenship status results from the person's naturalisation,*
>
> *(b) the Secretary of State is satisfied that the deprivation is conducive to the public good because the person, while having that citizenship status, has conducted him or herself in a manner which is seriously prejudicial to the vital interests of the United*

> *Kingdom, any of the Islands, or any British overseas territory, and*
>
> *(c) the Secretary of State has reasonable grounds for believing that the person is able, under the law of a country or territory outside the United Kingdom, to become a national of such a country or territory.*

Conducive to the public good meaning

'*Conducive to the public good*' is not defined in the BNA 1981. Nor is there any provision in section 40 requiring the Secretary of State to have regard to a series of obligatory considerations in determining what is conducive to the public good.

The Secretary of State's policy relating to the exercise of the power conferred by section 40(2) is however set out in the '*Deprivation of British citizenship*' guidance for caseworkers. The guidance defines for caseworkers what is meant by, '*conducive to the public good*' in section 40(2) as being:

> *""Conducive to the public good" means that it is in the public interest to deprive an individual of British citizenship because of their conduct and/or the threat they pose to the UK. Examples of when a person can be deprived of British citizenship on the ground that it is conducive to the public good include, but are not limited to:*
>
> - *the interests of national security, for reasons relating to terrorism, hostile state activity, or any other reason*
> - *where the person has been involved in serious organised crime*

- *where the person has been involved in war crimes, crimes against humanity, or other unacceptable behaviour"*

Deprivation is therefore likely to be pursued as 'Conducive to the Public Good' where it is considered by the Secretary of State that an individual has been involved in:

(i) Acts of terrorism

(ii) Espionage

(iii) Serious organised crime

(iv) War crimes

(v) Unacceptable behaviour

Decision made under section 40(2) will more usually be taken on the basis of involvement with terrorism or espionage. Such behaviour is likely to be obvious to the decision maker as requiring deprivation for the public good.

However, a case not involving terrorism or espionage is **Ahmed and Others (deprivation of citizenship) (Pakistan)**[6] which concerned an appeal brought by four men who had been convicted of what was described as very grave sexual offences, undertaken in the context of a conspiracy to commit them, between the spring of 2008 and the spring of 2010. Their criminal behaviour was summarised by the Upper Tribunal as "*the grooming and sexual exploitation of a number of girls in their early teens, in the area of Rochdale and Oldham*". The appellant's convictions included various inter-related offences: the trafficking of children for sexual exploitation, rape, conspiracy to engage in sexual

6 [2017] UKUT 118 (IAC)

activity with children and sexual coercion and their sentences ranged from 6 to 19 years imprisonment.

All of the appellants were of Pakistani nationality and had acquired British citizenship by naturalisation. The Secretary of State sought to deprive the appellants of their British citizenship under section 40(2) of the British Nationality Act 1981 stating that it was conducive to the public good for them to lose their British citizenship. The appellants' convictions were the sole basis for the Secretary of State's decisions made under section 40(2).

The Upper Tribunal at paragraph 61 set out that, "*chapter 55*[7] *of the " UK Visas and Immigration Nationality Instructions: Volume 1" was plainly a material consideration to be weighed by the decision maker in all of these cases*". It had not been argued by the appellant's that the guidance had not been followed in terms of what was meant by '*conducive to the public good*', but rather that the offending did not fall within the meaning of '*serious organised crime*'. The Upper Tribunal disagreed, concluding it was reasonably open to the Secretary of State and the First-Tier Tribunal to have concluded that the offending fell into '*serious organised crime*' and that deprivation was therefore warranted under section 40(2).

The UT noted the following useful points at paragraph 61 of the judgment:

> *"(i) Section 40(2) of the 1981 Act confers on the Secretary of State a discretionary power to deprive a person of British citizenship.*
>
> *(ii) The statutory pre-condition to the exercise of this power is that the Secretary of State must be " satisfied" that " deprivation is conducive to the public good". This is a paradigm public law empowering provision. Thus in every case the Secretary of State's decision, inter alia, must not lapse into irrationality, must be*

7 The guidance in force at the time

> *informed by taking into account all material considerations (which include chapter 55) and must not be contaminated by the intrusion of immaterial considerations. This is not an exhaustive checklist.*
>
> *(iii) While Chapter 55 purports to supply a definition of " conducive to the public good" this cannot have the effect of supplementing the statute. It belongs purely to the realm of a legislation related policy.*
>
> *(iv) Paragraph 55.4.4 does no more than indicate the kind of cases in which the statutory power might be exercised and it does so without prescription. It does not purport to be exhaustive or comprehensive. This is particularly clear from the words " unacceptable behaviours". It is difficult to conceive of a looser, more open – ended linguistic formula. Fundamentally, we consider that paragraph 55.4.4 simply provides case workers with some basic guidance as to how the statutory power might be exercised*
>
> *(v) The exercise of the statutory power in every case must be harmonious with the statutory language, accord with the underlying legislative intention and further the policy and objects of the statute, duly infused with the avoidance of fetter of discretion in accordance with the hallowed British Oxygen principle (British Oxygen v Board of Trade [1971] AC 610)."*

The case was unsuccessfully appealed to the Court of Appeal by three of the four appellants, the decision in respect of their appeal is set out in **Aziz v SSHD**[8]. At paragraph 35 of the decision the Court of Appeal emphasised that having issued policy guidance in respect of how the discretion under section 40(2) of the BNA 1981 would be exercised, the Secretary of State (and the FTT) were bound in law to apply the policy

8 [2018] EWCA Civ 1884

guidance, or to say that they were departing from it, giving rational and defensible reasons for doing so.

The Court of Appeal also set out that if what were said in the guidance to be '*unacceptable behaviours*' was to be relied upon by a decision maker for a conclusion that deprivation was conducive to the public good, "*an evaluative judgment would be required in relation to whether the conduct of the appellants fell within those words*". As the Upper Tribunal observed, "i*t is difficult to conceive of a looser, more open – ended linguistic formula*" than the phrase '*unacceptable behaviours.*' It's a phrase that may therefore see increasing reliance by the Secretary of State in seeking to deprive individual of their British nationality where behaviour is considered to be unacceptable.

Section 40(4) – stateless

Section 40(4) of the BNA 1981 imposes a restriction, or a limitation, on the power of the Secretary of State to make a deprivation order under section 40(2) of the BNA 1981. The subsection provides, subject to section 40(4A), that:

> *"(4) The Secretary of State may not make a deprivation order under subsection (2) if he is satisfied that the order would make a person stateless."*

In **Pham v Secretary of State for the Home Department**[9] the Supreme Court noted that the term "stateless" in section 40(4) has the same meaning as in article 1(1) of the 1954 Convention relating to the Status of Stateless Persons. The definition of statelessness as set out in article 1 of the UN Convention is a person *"who is not considered as a national by any State under the operation of its law"*. The Court accepted at paragraph 38 that the question arising under article 1(1) of the Convention is not necessarily to be decided solely by reference to the text of the nationality

9 [2015] UKSC 19 (25 March 2015)

legislation of the state in question, but that reference may also be made to the practice of the government, even if not subject to effective challenge in the courts in terms of how the law operates in practice. Expert evidence may therefore often be required to address whether in fact or practice an individual would be a national of a particular country.

Prior to the enactment of section 40(4A), the Supreme Court held in **Secretary of State for the Home Department v Al-Jedda**[10] that what matters is whether the person holds another nationality as of the date of the order for deprivation; that the person is entitled to another nationality upon application, with no need for discretion to be exercised in their favour, is immaterial.

Section 40(4A) sets out that section 40(4) does not prevent the Secretary of State from making an order under subsection (2) where citizenship resulted from naturalisation and subsection 40(4A)(b) and (c) apply. Namely that the deprivation is conducive to the public good because the person, has conducted themselves whilst a British national in a manner which is seriously prejudicial to the vital interests of the UK, any of the Islands, or any British overseas territory, and the Secretary of State has reasonable grounds for believing that the person is able to become a national of another country or territory. In the case of **Al-Jedda**, that the appellant was entitled to apply for Iraqi nationality would have brought him with section 40(4A).

The Explanatory Notes accompanying the Immigration Act 2014 which introduced section 40(4A) state that:

> *"[section 40(4A)] is intended to be more closely aligned with the 1961 UN Convention on the Prevention of Stateless, which allowed states to declare on ratifying the Convention that they retained the right to detain a person and render them stateless in specific circumstances." (Paragraph 406)*

---

[10] [2013] UKSC 62 (9 October 2013)

Although section 40(4) has been described as creating a condition precedent to the making of an order, the Court of Appeal in **E3 & Ors v Secretary of State for the Home Department [2023]**[11] said it is more accurate to describe section 40(4) as a limitation on the circumstances in which the power under section 40(2) may be exercised. The Secretary of State must consider whether a deprivation order would render a person stateless. If the Secretary of State "is satisfied" that the order would render the person stateless, she cannot make the order. If she is not satisfied of that fact, she may exercise the power to make a deprivation order.

Importantly, the Court of Appeal in **E3 & Ors** noted that the limitation under section 40(4) is expressed by reference to whether the Secretary of State is satisfied of a certain state of affairs. Importantly, it is not dependent on whether or not the state of affairs exists. The Court observed that the subsection "*does not provide that the Secretary of State may not make a deprivation order "if the order would render a person stateless"; it provides that the Secretary of State may not make such an order "if he is satisfied" that the order would render the person stateless*".

The state of mind of the Secretary of State has to be based upon the evidence available to them at the time that they decide to make a deprivation order. Therefore, before making a deprivation order the Secretary of State has to be satisfied that the order will not render the individual stateless, this requires a degree of investigation by the Home Office. It is this investigation that is said to provide the necessary safeguard in respect of an individual's rights. Longmore LJ in **Hashi v SSHD**[12] observed that it is a comparatively easy burden for the Secretary of State to discharge in order to demonstrate that they are satisfied the individual will not be rendered stateless by the decision. Once the Secretary of State has demonstrated that they are satisfied the deprivation order will not render the individual stateless, the burden of proving that the individual will be rendered stateless by the deprivation order is on the

---

[11] EWCA Civ 26 (17 January 2023)

[12] [2016] EWCA Civ 1136

individual (*see* **The Secretary of State for the Home Department v E3 & Anor (21 November 2019)**)[13].

In **E3 (17 January 2023)** the Court of Appeal accepted that there is significance in the use of the words "is satisfied" in section 40(4) of the BNA 1981. The Court summarised the significance as the deprivation order will be lawful if the Secretary of State exercises the power in circumstances where she is satisfied, on the material before her, that the person would not be stateless as a result. The Court distinguished the concerns expressed by Lord Wilson in **Al-Jedda** as to whether the phrase "is satisfied" had any meaning. The Court in E3 noted that Lord Wilson was dealing with the meaning of "is satisfied" in a different historical context. The issue in that case was whether the Secretary of State could make a deprivation order if, at the time, it was open to a person to apply for citizenship of another state. It was in that context, the Court observed, that Lord Wilson did not consider the words "is satisfied" could be afforded significance. The Court of Appeal held that in the present context, the lawfulness of the deprivation order does depend upon the state of mind of the Secretary of State, not the actual fact of 'statelessness' itself.

The Court of Appeal therefore set out that the limitation imposed on the Secretary of State is that she may not exercise the power to deprive a person of his status as a British national if she is satisfied that would render the individual stateless. If she is not satisfied of that fact, the limitation on her powers does not apply and her order will be lawful. The Court of Appeal accordingly held that the phrase "is satisfied" does have a significant role in the operation of section 40 of the BNA 1981 and is distinct from the individual is actually rendered stateless. That distinction is important when considering the consequences of decisions to deport and the scope of successful appeals.

---

[13] [2019] EWCA Civ 2020

The use of the Secretary of State's power under section 40(2) is therefore likely to be exercised against individuals that have acquired British citizenship through naturalisation and retain their original nationality or where the individual is, for example, a 2nd or 3rd generation immigrant and holds another nationality through their parents or grandparents. The later of those two means that the exercise of the power under section 40(2) can be taken against an individual who is a British citizen by birth (see for example case of Shamima Begum). In contrast decision under s.40(4A) apply only to those who naturalised as British by virtue of subsection (a).

When assisting individuals, facing a possible deprivation decision under section 40(2) it is important to have regard to any other possible nationalities they may hold and if they naturalised as British, any nationalities they might be entitled to obtain. Expert evidence on the individual country's law and operation is likely to be required and is something to perhaps consider from an early stage.

CHAPTER FIVE

SECTION 40(3) – FRAUD, FALSE REPRESENTATION & CONCEALMENT

Section 40(3) of the British Nationality Act 1981 'the BNA 1981' is the more common power exercised by the Secretary of State to deprive an individual of their British citizenship. Section 40(3) provides the Secretary of State with a discretionary power to deprive a person of their citizenship which was obtained as the result of registration or naturalisation, if the Secretary of State is satisfied it was obtained by means of:

(a) fraud,

(b) false representation, or

(c) concealment of a material fact.

Unlike the exercise of the power under section 40(2) a decision cannot be taken by the Secretary of State against an individual who was born a British citizen. The limitation to deprivation on conducive grounds under section 40(4), that a decision cannot be taken if that would render the individual stateless, does not apply to section 40(3). The reason for the distinction is perhaps obvious, a decision to deprive under section 40(3) arises due to the conduct of the individual in obtaining their British citizenship.

The fraud, false representation, or concealment can have taken place prior to the enactment of the BNA 1981 and section 40(6) of the Act provides that:

> *"(6) Where a person acquired a citizenship status by the operation of a law which applied to him because of his registration or naturalisation under an enactment having effect before commencement, the Secretary of State may by order deprive the person of the citizenship status if the Secretary of State is satisfied that the registration or naturalisation was obtained by means of—*
>
> *(a) fraud,*
>
> *(b) false representation, or*
>
> *(c) concealment of a material fact."*

As such historical registration or naturalisation would not prevent the Secretary of State from being able to exercise their power to deprive an individual of their citizenship. Time is therefore not a bar to action being considered and taken.

Definitions

Similar to the meaning of '*conducive to the public good*' under section 40(2) the three different criteria set out in section 40(3) are not defined in the BNA 1981. Nor is there any provision in section 40 requiring the Secretary of State to have regard to a series of obligatory considerations in determining what is meant by those terms.

The Secretary of State's policy relating to the exercise of the power conferred by section 40(3) is however set out in the Home Office's caseworker guidance, 'Deprivation of British citizenship' which defines them as follows:

'False representation' is defined in the guidance as "*a representation which was deliberately and dishonestly made on the applicant's part, that is where an innocent mistake would not give rise to a decision to deprive under this provision. The false representation must have had a direct bearing on the application.*"

'Concealment of any material fact' is defined in the guidance as a "*deliberate operative concealment rather than an innocent omission*". That is explained as a "*concealment practised by the applicant*" which is deliberate and must have had a direct bearing on the decision to register or to issue a certificate of naturalisation.

'Fraud' is defined in the guidance as encompassing "*either of the above.*" Unhelpfully it is not defined beyond that in the guidance. It can of course be understood by its ordinary everyday meaning.

The definition of '*false representation*' requires dishonesty and it can reasonably be assumed that take at face value that 'fraud' also requires dishonesty. There is, however, no requirement in the definition set out in the guidance that '*concealment of any material fact*' was done so dishonestly, although it must have been deliberate.

Relevant Fact

A wide variety of false or concealed facts may lead to consideration of deprivation. As noted above section 40(6) provides for deprivation where the fraud, false representation or concealment occurred before the commencement of the BNA 1981. The guidance emphasis the point that "*length of residence in the UK alone will not normally be a reason not to deprive a person of their citizenship*", but should be taken into account when considering whether deprivation is reasonable and, in respect of any ECHR considerations, proportionate.

The guidance sets out that relevant factors which are said to be material to the acquisition of citizenship are those that if, the fact been known at the time the application was considered, they would have affected the decision to grant citizenship.

A non-exhausted list of possible factors is set out in the guidance as:

(i) Undisclosed convictions

(ii) other information which would have affected a person's ability to meet the good character requirement in place at the time the person applied for citizenship

(iii) A marriage/civil partnership which is found to be invalid or void, and so would have affected a person's ability to meet the requirements as a married person

(iv) False details given in relation to an immigration or asylum application, which led to that status being given to a person who would not otherwise have qualified, and so would have affected a person's ability to meet the residence and/or good character requirements for naturalisation or registration

In considering the facts, there needs to have been an intent on the part of the individual to have deceived the Home Office. The guidance makes clear that "*an innocent error or genuine omission should not lead to deprivation.*" A deliberate abuse in the application process may however result in deprivation.

<u>Material</u>

False details given in relation to a past immigration or asylum application which might be material include the individual's name, date of birth, nationality, or place of birth. Importantly, the guidance states that "*if the fraud, false representation or concealment of material fact did not have a direct bearing on the grant of citizenship, it will not be appropriate to pursue deprivation action*". Where deprivation is being taken on the basis of information provided in respect of or given in a previous application, it is important to obtain the individual's Home Office file. Notes appertaining to the decision to grant leave may well be relevant to the question of whether what is said to be fraudulent had '*a direct bearing*' on the grant. The importance of this can be seen in the guidance itself which states by way of example, "*...a person may have previously been granted settlement under a concession where identity and nationality were not qualifying criteria. Despite the fact that they used a false identity at the time, the fraud cannot be said to be material to the grant of settlement. It might therefore not have been material to the grant of citizenship.*"

Some non-exhaustive examples for when it may not have had a direct bearing on the outcome. include:

(i) where a person acquired ILR under a concession (e.g. the family ILR concession), the fact it could be shown they had lied during an asylum claim may be irrelevant.

(ii) A person may use a different name if they wish and unless it conceals criminality or other information relevant to an assessment of their good character, or immigration history in another identity it is not material to the acquisition of ILR or citizenship.

In **Sleiman (deprivation of citizenship; conduct: Lebanon)**[14] the Upper Tribunal considered the question of materiality. The Upper Tribunal held the impugned behaviour must be 'directly material' to the decision to grant citizenship. The headnote of the decision sets out that:

> *"In an appeal against a decision to deprive a person of a citizenship status, in assessing whether the appellant obtained registration or naturalisation "by means of" fraud, false representation, or concealment of a material fact, the impugned*

14 [2017] UKUT 367 (IAC) (19 July 2017)

> *behaviour must be directly material to the decision to grant citizenship."*

The appellant in **Sleiman** lied about his age when claiming asylum. As a result, he was granted limited leave as an unaccompanied child by the Secretary of State. On turning 18, he applied for further leave to remain, but there was a delay in the Home Office making a decision h and his case was ultimately considered and granted under the 'legacy' process, resulting in him being granted indefinite leave to remain. A subsequent application for naturalisation was successful and he became a British citizen.

Whilst travelling abroad he encounter difficulties and his British passport was surrendered to the authorities in Hong Kong. He then travelled to China where he contacted the British embassy for assistance. He provided a copy of his Lebanese passport to the embassy which had his correct date of birth. He was able to obtain an emergency travel document and returned back to the UK. As a result of the disclosure of his Lebanese passport the incorrect, date of birth used during his asylum claim was discovered. The Secretary of State made a decision to deprive him of his British Citizenship on the basis that it was obtained fraudulently.

The Upper Tribunal in considering the appeal took into account what was set out in the guidance. The Upper Tribunal observed that the phrase 'direct bearing' in the guidance was consistent with "by means of" in the BNA 1981. The Upper Tribunal notes that clearly there must be some causative link between the action(s) or omission of the individual and the obtaining of citizenship.

At paragraph 60 of the determination the Upper Tribunal set out:

> *"The phrase "direct bearing" suggests that in cases where the fraud etc. only has an indirect bearing on the grant of citizenship, deprivation action would not be appropriate. This, it seems to me, is consistent with the phrase "by means of" in s.40 (3). Furthermore, under the "Definitions" in the NI's,*

> *"Concealment of any material fact" (although s.40 (3) itself reads "concealment of a material fact"), is described as meaning " operative concealment i.e. the concealment practised by the applicant must have had a direct bearing on the decision to register or, as the case may be, to issue a certificate of naturalisation" (emphasis as in original)."*

At paragraph 62 the Upper Tribunal concluded that "*the impugned behaviour must be directly material to the decision to grant citizenship*".

It should be borne in mind that the Upper Tribunal's decision in **Sleiman** was considered in the context of the Tribunal having a wider jurisdiction to determine appeals and where the Tribunal's role was to decide for itself whether the Secretary of State had exercised her discretion correctly when deciding to deprive. Therefore, the Tribunal had to decide for itself whether the condition precedent in section 40(3) was met. The approach the Tribunal is able to take post the decision in **Begum v SSHD**[15] in a deprivation appeal is seemingly limited to consideration of whether public law errors have been made by the Secretary of State (see later chapters).

The question in many cases that individuals will need to consider addressing is whether or not the act or omission was '*directly material*' to the grant of British citizenship. Of assistance in answering that question will be the Home Office's casework notes from the time. A decision which did not take into account a file note making it clear that the issue was not material would likely be a material error.

The guidance sets out a number of circumstances in which deprivation under section 40(3) will generally not be pursued which are:

(i) Fraud postdates the application for British citizenship;

[15] [2021] UKSC 7

(ii) The individual was a minor at the date they applied for British citizenship;

(iii) The individual was minor when they acquired ILR and the fraud, false representations or concealment arose at that time and the leave led to the individual obtaining British citizenship.

The guidance does however emphasis that the three points above would not prevent deprivation being pursued where it is "*in the public interest to deprive*" the individual of their citizenship.

Complicit

In some circumstances, for example a spouse, it will be necessary for Secretary of State to consider whether an individual who has benefit from fraud, false representations or concealment in obtaining their citizenship had been complicit in those actions. The Secretary of State takes a different view dependent on the age of the individual.

In respect of children, the Secretary of State will generally assume that they were not complicit in any deception by their parent or guardian. That includes those who were granted discretionary leave until their 18th birthday having entered the UK as a sole minor who could not be returned because of a lack of reception arrangements. However, where a minor submits an application for asylum or other form of leave which maintains a fraud, false representation or concealment of material fact which they adopted whilst a minor, after they have turned 18 years old, they will be treated by the Secretary of State as complicit.

In contrast to children, all adults will be viewed by the Secretary of State as legally responsible for their own citizenship applications, even where they are made as part of a family application. In respect of adults, complicity will normally therefore be assumed unless sufficient evidence in mitigation is provided, by the individual in question, to the Secretary of State as part of the investigations process. Evidence of the individual's mental health or of a coercive partner might be relevant to the Secretary of State's considerations in supporting an argument that the individual was not complicit in the fraud. For adults, the fact that they were advised by a relative or agent to give false information may not be treated by the Secretary of State as an indication that they were not complicit in the deception. The guidance goes on to set out a number of factors which may amount to mitigation and those that will not.

Other considerations

In reaching a decision to deprive an individual under section 40(3) of their British citizenship the guidance sets out a number of other factors which should be considered:

(i) Whether the decision to deprive is a balanced and reasonable step

(ii) Any mitigating circumstances

(iii) The evidence the decision is being made on; and

(iv) Whether the decision breaches the individual's rights under the European convention on Human Rights 'ECHR'

As the power to deprive is a discretionary one, it is important for individuals to have regard to the above factors when making representations and whether or not the Secretary of State has taken them into account in reaching a decision to deprive.

Balanced and reasonable step?

Consideration needs to be given by the Secretary of State as to whether deprivation would be seen to be a balanced and reasonable step to take, taking into account the seriousness of the fraud, misrepresentation or concealment, the level of evidence for this, and what information was available to the Secretary of State at the time of consideration. Importantly, evidence that was before the Secretary of State at the time of application but was disregarded or mishandled should not in general be used at a later stage to deprive an individual of their British citizenship. As with considering whether the fact was material to the grant, access to the Home Office records will be useful in understanding what the Secretary of State knew or ought to have known. For example, had the fact already been drawn to the Secretary of State's attention but disregarded at a previous stage. However, evidence known to the Secretary of State but disregarded or mishandled will not prevent deprivation where it is in the public interest to deprive.

Mitigation

The guidance requires the decision maker to consider any mitigating circumstances. As noted above, adults are expected to take responsibility for their own applications, in particular the information contained within. The following are therefore set out as examples which will not be considered as mitigating factors:

(i) Where the applicant claims that a family member acted on their behalf

(ii) Where the applicant claims that a representative or interpreter advised them to provide false details

(iii) Where an applicant claims that he or she was coerced into providing false information or concealing a fact, but has since had the opportunity to advise the Home Office of the correct position but failed to do so

Examples of factors that may be considered mitigating are given as:

(i) Where there is evidence of some form of mental or physical impairment that can clearly be shown to have impacted on the subject's judgement at the time the material fraud took place

(ii) Where there is evidence of some form of coercion that indicates that the subject was not able to make independent decisions at the time the material fraud took place

If seeking to rely on either of those two factors, it is necessary to establish that they indicate a "*lack of free will and/or sound judgement*" on the part of the individual. Supportive evidence is required by the Secretary of State. As such a statement from the individual will not of itself be sufficient for a decision to deprive being unreasonable or unbalanced, based on an individual's health or coercion. Medial evidence from either the individual's doctor or other relevant health professional would be required in order to establish that their health impacted on their free will or judgement.

Evidence

The evidence relied upon by the Secretary of State to establish the fraud, false representation or concealment needs to be sufficient. The guidance makes clear that the Secretary of State does not wish to pursue deprivation against individuals where it is likely to be overturned on appeal, owing to it not being an ineffective use of public resources.

The guidance therefore poses the following questions for decision makers to consider:

(i) Does the evidence presented as part of the investigation process meet the necessary standard of proof?

(ii) Is there an admission of guilt or strong evidence from a third party of action which suggests guilt?

(iii) Is the evidence weak or based on hearsay and therefore likely to be easily challenged?

When representing individuals, it might be worthwhile taking into account the above questions in order to challenge the Secretary of State on the quality of evidence being relied upon to purse deprivation. In particular, is there an actual '*admission of guilt*' or merely an acknowledgement they have previously been known by a different name. Similarly, if dishonesty is required, is that actually made out on the evidence. What is the source of the evidence relied upon by the Secretary of State and how reliable is it.

Article 8 of the ECHR

In reaching a decision under section 40(3) the Secretary of State will consider the impact of deprivation on the individual's rights under the ECHR. In particular whether deprivation would interfere with the individual's private and family life. If it would, the Secretary of State will need to consider whether a decision to deprive would nevertheless be proportionate. A decision to deprive is separate from a decision to remove an individual. Deprivation may well be a proportionate outcome, but removal may not, leading to a later grant of leave to remain.

CHAPTER SIX

PROCEDURE

There is no specific time limit within which deprivation procedures must be initiated. A person to whom section 40 of British Nationality Act 1981 'the BNA 1981' applies remains indefinitely liable to deprivation, under either ground.

Investigation

Prior to reaching a decision on deprivation there will usually be an investigation by the Secretary of State to establish whether or not the discretionary power to deprive the individual of their British citizenship should be exercised. Often concerns will be raised with the Secretary of State arising from new information; for example, if an individual applies to amend their details on their British passport (name, date or place of birth) or applies for another family member providing details previously unknown to the Secretary of State.

An investigation letter will be sent to the individual setting out the basis of the allegation and the evidence collected to support the proposed decision to deprive. At this stage a final decision to deprive will not have been taken. The Secretary of State will usually invite a response from the individual in respect of the possibility their citizenship maybe revoked. This will, for example, provide for an opportunity for the individual to respond to allegations of fraud, false representation or concealment. It also provides an opportunity to offer any mitigating circumstances that may explain the alleged actions. The individual will be given 21 calendar days to provide a response to the investigation letter. Extension requests can be made but generally the maximum period given to respond by the Secretary of State will be 3 months.

Decision To Deprive

As there is no specific time limit within which a deprivation decision may be made, an individual to whom section 40 of the BNA 1981 applies remains indefinitely liable to deprivation. However, the factors surrounding any delay in making the decision to deprive will need to be considered[16].

Once the Secretary of State has made a decision to deprive, section 40(5) of the BNA 1981 requires a person to normally be given written notice of the decision to make an order for deprivation, including the reasons for deprivation and about their rights to appeal the decision. However, in some circumstances a decision to deprive may be taken without giving notice.

Under Regulation 10 of the British Nationality (General) Regulations 2003, the deprivation notice can be served by the following means:

- by post to an address in the UK or overseas, via normal or recorded delivery
- by fax
- by email
- by document exchange
- by courier
- by hand

A deprivation notice may also be served on the individual's representative or, if the person is under 18, on their parent or guardian, or to the last

[16] See for example Laci v Secretary of State for the Home Department [2021] EWCA Civ 769

known address for the individual or their representative. The Home Office must keep a record on the file or on CID/Atlas when a deprivation notice has been sent, to whom and by what method of delivery. The deprivation notices will be deemed served within the following timescales:

- if sent by post to an address in the UK, 2 days after it is sent
- if sent by post to an address overseas, 28 days after it is sent
- where it is sent by recorded delivery, when the postal record shows it is delivered
- where the notice is sent by document exchange, on the day after the day on which it is sent
- if sent by any other means, when it is delivered or sent

Once notice has been given of a deprivation decision, a deprivation order, which is what legally removes a person's British citizenship, can be made.

Deprivation without giving notice

Under section 40(5A) of the BNA 1981 the Secretary of State may deprive an individual of their British citizenship under section 40(2), section 40(3) or section 40(6) without giving notice. This may be where there is insufficient information needed to be able to give notice or where it is considered necessary in the interests of national security or the investigation or prosecution of organised or serious crime.

Where the decision to deprive is being made under section 40(2) on the ground that it is conducive to the public good, paragraph 1(1) of Schedule 4A to the BNA 1981 requires an application to be made to the Special Immigration Appeals Commission (SIAC) before a deprivation order is made. Paragraph 1(2) of Schedule 4A to the BNA 1981 requires the Secretary of State to make an application to SIAC within 7 days of the deprivation order being made. Schedule 4A also sets out the requirement to regularly review cases where a decision to deprive on the ground that it is conducive to the public good is made without first giving notice.

In all cases where the Secretary of State has not given notice of a decision to deprive, under section 40(5D) of the BNA, late notice must be given to the individual deprived of their citizenship if they later make contact directly with the Home Office.

Section 55

Section 55 of the Borders, Citizenship and Immigration Act 2009 requires the Home Office to carry out its existing functions in a way that takes into account the need to safeguard and promote the welfare of children in the UK. Where there are children involved, the Secretary of State will have to have regard to their best interest when considering whether or not to deprive an individual of their citizenship.

Out of the UK

An order for deprivation takes effect immediately. Appeals against deprivation decisions are not suspensive. As a result, if the individual is outside of the UK at the time the decision is made, they will need to seek entry clearance to return.

In **Islam, R (On the Application Of) v Secretary of State for the Home Department**[17] the applicant sought through a claim for judicial review to challenge the Secretary of State's decision to deprive his son of British

17 [2019] EWHC 2169 (Admin) (07 August 2019)

citizen due to him having joined ISIL. He sought an order requiring the Home Office to return his son back to the UK.

It was argued relying on the decision of the House of Lords in **R (Al-Skeini) v. Secretary of State for Defence**[18] that domestic legislation will not generally operate on its subjects beyond the country's territorial limits, and that the British Nationality Act 1981 therefore does not apply to a British subject outside the United Kingdom. Further, that Regulation 10 of the British Nationality (General) Regulations 2003 should be construed that it does not apply extra-territorially.

In addressing the argument Mr Justice Pepperall considered there was no merit in those arguments. He concluded the construction point was hopeless, in that regulation 10(5)(e) clearly envisaged that notice could be given to a citizen while they are overseas. Further, there is nothing in s.41, under which the regulations were made, or otherwise in the BNA 1981to prevent notice from being served on a citizen who is overseas. It is therefore safest to ensure that individuals ae not out of the UK when deprivation of citizenship is a real possibility.

[18] [2008] 1 AC 153

CHAPTER SEVEN

RIGHT OF APPEAL

An individual has a right of appeal against a decision notified to them under section 40(5) of the British Nationality Act 1981 'the BNA 1981'. Section 40A(1) of the BNA 1981 provides that:

> *"(1) A person who is given notice under section 40(5) of a decision to make an order in respect of him under section 40 may appeal against the decision to the First-tier Tribunal."*

The venue for the appeal against the decision will therefore normally be the First-Tier Tribunal (Immigration & Asylum Chamber). However, if the Secretary of State certifies the decision to deprive an individual of their British citizenship pursuant to section 40A(2) of the BNA 1981 the right of appeal lies instead to the to the Special Immigration Appeals Commission ("SIAC"), under section 2B of the Special Immigration Appeals Commission Act 1997.

A certificate pursuant to section 40A(2) of the BNA 1981 will be issued if the decision to deprive had been made wholly or partly in reliance on information which in the Secretary of State's opinion should not be made public either:

(a) in the interests of national security,

(b) in the interests of the relationship between the United Kingdom and another country, or

(c) otherwise in the public interest.

Nationality and Borders Act 2022

Sections 10(6) to (8) of the Nationality and Borders Act 2022 the 2022 Act came into force on 28 April 2022. They deal with rights of appeal in circumstances where there has been a failure by the Secretary of State to comply with the duty under section 40(5) of the BNA 1981.

Section 10(8) of the 2022 Act provides that:

> *"(8) A person may appeal against a decision to make an order to which subsection (6) applies as if notice of the decision had been given to the person under section 40(5) of the 1981 Act on the day on which the order was made or purportedly made."*

Section 10(6) provides:

> *"(6) A failure to comply with the duty under section 40(5) of the 1981 Act in respect of a pre-commencement deprivation order does not affect, and is to be treated as never having affected, the validity of the order."*

A 'pre-commencement deprivation order' is defined by subsection 7 as:

> *"(7) In subsection (6), "pre-commencement deprivation order" means an order made or purportedly made under section 40 of the 1981 Act before the coming into force of subsections (2) to (5) (whether before or after the coming into force of subsection (6))."*

The introduction of sections 10(6) to (8) aims to protect from the consequence of decisions for which proper notice had not been given as held in the judgment in **R (OAO D4) v SSHD**[19] The judgment was upheld by the Court of Appeal[20].

Onward appeals

An onward appeal from the First-Tier tribunal (IAC) would lie to the Upper Tribunal (IAC). Whilst an appeal from SIAC lies to the Court of Appeal.

Consequence of appeal

As originally enacted, section 40A(6) of the BNA 1981 provided that appeals under either section 40A(1) of the BNA 1981 or section 2B of the 1997 Act were suspensive, and that no order depriving a person of citizenship could take effect while an appeal was pending. But that provision was repealed by paragraph 4 of Schedule 2 to the Asylum and Immigration (Treatment of Claimants, etc.) Act 2004 with the effect that a deprivation order now takes effect from the moment that it is made, but that order remains subject to a (non-suspensive) right of appeal.

---

19 [2021] EWHC 2179 (Admin)

20 in D4 [2022] EWCA Civ 33 (26 January 2022)

CHAPTER EIGHT

SIAC

The Special Immigration Appeals Commission 'SIAC' will usually be required to resolve either an application made by the Secretary of State to not give notice of a decision to deprive on the ground that it is conducive to the public good or an appeal brought by individuals under section 2B of Special Immigration Appeals Commission Act 1997.

Decision to deprive on the ground that it is conducive to the public good, without giving notice

Section 7 of The Special Immigration Appeals Commission (Procedure) (Amendment) Rules 2023 inserts Part 4A to the Special Immigration Appeals Commission (Procedure) Rules 2003 (the procedure rules) and sets out the process to be followed when the Secretary of State makes an application to SIAC. An application to SIAC can be made by the Secretary of State in advance of making the deprivation order, where there is an intent to make a decision to deprive on the ground that it is conducive to the public good, without giving notice. However, where a decision is made to make a deprivation order whilst SIAC is still considering the application, the Secretary of State must inform SIAC of this development.

Paragraph 1(2) of Schedule 4A requires the Secretary of State to make an application to SIAC within 7 days of making a deprivation order. The Secretary of State may also make an application to SIAC at any time for fresh consideration of a decision to rely on section 40(5A) if there is a material change in the circumstances or there is further evidence the Secretary of State seeks to rely upon.

The application to SIAC must set out the reasons and considerations made to deprive the individual of their British citizenship without giving them notice of the decision.

Determination of the Special Immigration Appeals Commission

Under Rule 25E of the procedure rules, SIAC is required to issue its determination within 14 days of receiving an application from the Secretary of State. Where SIAC determines that the Secretary of State's view is obviously flawed, the Secretary of State must, within 14 days, either:

- give the individual notice of the decision to deprive
- withdraw the deprivation order
- make a fresh application for consideration by SIAC

Fresh applications to SIAC however, can only be made by the Secretary of State where there is a material change to the circumstances of the case and/or where the Secretary of State wishes to provide further evidence to support their position.

Review of decisions not to give notice

Paragraph 2 of Schedule 4A to the BNA provides for a period of review of cases where notice of a deprivation decision is not given. In cases where SIAC has determined that the Secretary of State's view is not obviously flawed, the first review period starts the day after the day on which SIAC first determined the application. Cases must be reviewed by the Secretary of State every 4 months, up to a maximum of 2 years.

During each four-month review period, the Secretary of State must actively review the circumstances of the case and decide whether any of the conditions in section 40(5A) of the BNA 1981 still apply or whether it is now appropriate to give late notice of the deprivation decision to the individual. Where a decision is made that notice should be given and none of the reasons in section 40(5A) of the BNA 1981 apply, the Secretary of State must give notice of the deprivation decision as soon as reasonably practical. Once notice is given, the requirement to review ends.

At the end of the final review period, two years after the original SIAC determination that the decision not to give notice was not obviously flawed, if the Secretary of State considers there is still a reason not to give notice in accordance with section 40(5A) of the BNA 1981, the Secretary of State must make a final application to SIAC. Once SIAC issues its determination, this ends the legal requirement on the Secretary of State to actively review the case.

Appeal Against Deprivation Decision to SIAC

Section 2B of Special Immigration Appeals Commission Act 1997 '1997 Act' provides that:

> *"A person may appeal to the Special Immigration Appeals Commission against a decision to make an order under section 40 of the British Nationality Act 1981 (c. 61) (deprivation of citizenship) if he is not entitled to appeal under section 40A(1) of that Act because of a certificate under section 40A(2) (and section 40A(3)(a) shall have effect in relation to appeals under this section)"*

SIAC is independent of the government and appeals will be heard by a senior judge and two other commission members. SIAC is a superior court of record.

An appeal against a decision to deprive an individual of their British citizenship will be heard by SIAC, where the Secretary of State has issued a certificate under section 40A(2) of the British Nationality Act 1981. A certificate will be issued where a decision was taken either wholly or in part on information that should not be made public for one of the three reasons set out in that section.

Closed material

Given the need for open justice, decisions made based on information that should not be made public, can make for difficult hearings. SIAC was introduced by the 1997 Act to provide for a partially closed hearing under UK law to try and deal with any difficulty in a fair and just manner.

Hearing can be split into open and closed parts. During the closed part of the hearing the appellant and their legal team are excluded. The non-disclosable secret evidence relied upon by the Secretary of State is considered in their absence. Section 6(1) of the 1997 Act, however, provides for the appointment of person, a 'Special Advocate', to represent the appellant's interests during parts of the hearing from which they and their representatives are excluded.

Special Advocates are appointed by the Attorney General in England and Wales (1997 Act section 6(2)(a)). An appointee is required to have a have a general qualification for the purposes of section 71 of the Courts and Legal Services Act 1990. They will also have been vetted by the Security Service, given the sensitive nature of the material they are likely to be exposed to. Although, the Special Advocate represents the interests of the appellant section 6(4) of the 1997 Act make clear that they are not responsible to the person whose interests they are appointed to represent.

Some discussions between, the appellant and their lawyers with the Special Advocate may be permissible in advance of the hearing. However, once the Special Advocate has seen the closed material, they can only communicate with the appellant and their lawyers, with the permission of the Secretary of State.

If SIAC determines that some of the evidence being heard in secret is in fact disclosable, it has the power to direct that evidence be considered in open session. At the conclusion of the hearing, the court will produce both a closed and an open judgment.

National Security Concerns

In cases involving issues of national security, SIAC must accord to the Secretary of State a large margin of judgment. That margin will be granted not only in relation to the reasonableness or rationality of the Secretary of State's assessments but also in relation to the court's consideration of the proportionality of executive actions: **R (Youssef) v Secretary of State for Foreign and Commonwealth Affairs**[21] (see paragraph 57). The limitations on judicial powers in the sphere of national security have been recently restated by the Supreme Court in **Begum** (see chapter 10).

In **Secretary of State for the Home Department v Rehman**[22], at paragraph 57, Lord Hoffmann compared the institutional competence of the Secretary of State and SIAC:

> *"Not only is the decision entrusted to the Home Secretary but he also has the advantage of a wide range of advice from people with day-to-day involvement in security matters which [SIAC], despite its specialist membership, cannot match".*

In **Secretary of State for the Home Department v P3**[23] Bean LJ, Elisabeth Laing LJ and Sir Stephen Irwin considered the effect of Begum. The main issue was the correct approach for SIAC to adopt to its function when considering the Secretary of State's assessment of the interests of

---

21 [2016] UKSC 1

22 [2003] 1 AC 153

23 [2021] EWCA Civ 1642

national security in a case raising Convention rights. Sir Stephen Irwin at paragraph 126 of the judgment agreeing with Elisabeth Laing LJ that in approaching the evaluation of the national security assessment of the Secretary of State, SIAC must pay real respect to that assessment. It is not, therefore, a permissible approach for SIAC simply to substitute its own views on national security. He held:

> *"...it is the function of SIAC to scrutinise all the evidence, OPEN and CLOSED, with a critical and expert intelligence, to test the approach and the evidence bearing on the assessment, both for and against the conclusions of the Secretary of State, and then applying due deference, to decide whether the conclusions of the Secretary of State were reasonable and, adopting the phrase of the Strasbourg Court, conformed with common sense. In doing so, SIAC is bound to show deference at all stages and at all levels, to the assessments of those responsible for making those assessments professionally. In matters of high policy, that deference will be effectively simply acceptance. At more granular levels, SIAC will ask questions and consider the detailed replies. Experience suggests these questions will be considered thoughtfully, and the answers very frequently persuasive. Proper deference there must be, but it does not amount to a simply supine acceptance of the conclusions advanced by the Secretary of State. I do not understand that to be in any way implied by the decisions in **Rehman** or **Begum**."*

In practical terms, therefore the threshold for judicial interference in National Security cases will be high. In **QX v Secretary of State for the Home Department (Rev1)**[24] Mrs Justice Farbey set out, "*the Secretary of State's institutional competence relates not only to her judgment of what amounts to a risk to national security but also to matters of the assessment of intelligence. The interpretation of any particular piece of intelligence and the factual conclusions that should be reached from the intelligence picture are*

24 [2022] EWHC 836 (Admin) (07 April 2022)

matters properly decided by people with day-to-day involvement in security matters. If the High Court were to piece together the intelligence incorrectly and reach erroneous findings of fact, the risk to national security would be obvious but would bring no opportunity for democratic accountability". She continued that Parliament has nonetheless entrusted judges to review the lawfulness of the exercise of intrusive executive discretions and it would be a derogation of judicial responsibility if the outcome of a review were to be a foregone conclusion.

Time limits for applying

The current time limits for bringing an appeal are set out in Rule 8 of the Special Immigration Appeals Commission (Procedure) Rules 2003 as amended and are currently:

Appellant's location	Time limit
In detention	5 working days
In the UK	10 days
Outside the UK	28 days

Where a decision is made to deprive a person of British citizenship without giving notice, under section 40A(2A) of the British Nationality Act 1981 the time limit for appealing does not start until the person is given notice of the deprivation decision. However, if the deprivation order was made prior to the commencement of section 10(2) to (5) of the Nationality and Borders Act 2022, under section 10(8) the time limit for appealing starts from the date of the deprivation order.

Lodging an appeal out of time

The Special Immigration Appeals Commission Practice Note on late and improperly instituted appeals sets out the approach that the Commission will take when dealing with appeals made out of time. The guidance reiterates that the Commission can only extend time for lodging an appeal if the Commission is satisfied, by reason of special circumstances, it would be unjust not to extend time (rule 8(5)). Paragraphs 16 through to 24 set out the Commission's expectations, in particular at paragraphs 19 an appellant's representatives realised that the appeal is late (or is likely to be late) they must apply expressly for an extension of time in the notice of appeal. That application must be supported, as soon as possible, by evidence (that is, a signed and dated witness statement) which explains what has happened during the period of any delay. Preparation of that witness statement should not further delay the lodging of the notice of appeal and should normally be provided within 14 days after the notice of appeal is lodged. The notice of appeal should however contain short grounds outlining the reasons for the delay.

Legislation And Rules

The relevant legislation and guidance to have regard to when conducting proceeding in SIAC include:

- Special Immigration Appeals Commission Act 1997
- Nationality, Immigration and Asylum Act 2002
- Special Immigration Appeals Commission Procedure Rules 2003
- Practice note for proceedings before SIAC

Outcomes

There is no express provision governing the powers of SIAC on an appeal. SIAC will, therefore, simply allow the appeal if it determines that a decision to make a deprivation order does result, for example, in the person being rendered stateless. SIAC does not have power to quash the decision to make the order, still less the order itself which is the legal measure bringing about the deprivation of citizenship (see paragraph 33 of **E3 & Ors v Secretary of State for the Home Department**[25]). Further steps will need to be taken by the Secretary of State to give effect to the finding by SIAC that a person is rendered stateless by the order. In particular, the Secretary of State will have to withdraw the decision, and the order, thereby removing the legal measure that deprives the individual of his status as a British citizen.

If the appeal is allowed on public law grounds, it will be for the Secretary of State to consider whether the failings can be remedied and if so, whether or not to make a further, but lawful, decision to deprive the individual of their British citizenship.

Costs

In **C7 v Secretary of State for the Home Department**[26] the appellant appealed to the Court of Appeal, against a decision of SIAC, refusing an order that the Secretary of State, pay the costs of the appellant's successful appeal to SIAC. The judge decided that SIAC did not have the power to make such an order and did not consider that the Secretary of State's conduct during the appeal had been unreasonable. The Court of Appeal on hearing an appeal against that decision held, among other things, that:

---

[25] [2023] EWCA Civ 26

[26] [2023] EWCA Civ 265 (13 March 2023)

(i) SIAC did not have an inherent power to award costs on an appeal under s2B of the Special Immigration Appeals Commission Act 1997;

(ii) SIAC did not have an implied power to award costs on such an appeal;

(iii) if, contrary to that view, SIAC did have a power to award costs, a judge is entitled to decide that he would only order the Secretary of State to pay costs if her conduct of the appeal was unreasonable and

(iv) a judge is also entitled to decide whether the Secretary of State's conduct of the appeal is unreasonable.

CHAPTER NINE

FIRST-TIER TRIBUNAL

Deprivation appeals, which have not been certified under section 40A of the British Nationality Act 1981 'BNA 1981' are heard in the Immigration Asylum Chamber of the First-Tier Tribunal.

Appeals will usually be heard by a single judge of the First-Tier Tribunal, who will be independent from the Secretary of State. The Secretary of State will usually be represented in the proceedings by a Home Office Presenting Officer, a Civil Servant rather than a qualified lawyer.

Process

A solicitor or an immigration adviser, appealing on behalf of an individual must appeal online using the MyHMCTS service, unless the individual is in detention. MyHMCTS is an online case management tool for solicitors and other legal professionals managed by HM Courts and Tribunals (HMCTS) and allows the submission, and management of appeals online.

If the individual is detained the appeal must be made using the paper appeal form. IAFT-5 where the appellant has been detained in prison (not an Immigration detention centre) and their decision letter was sent by the Home Office. Where the appellant has been detained in an immigration detention centre and their decision letter was sent by the Home Office form IAFT-DIA should be used.

Appeals through the MyHMCTS portal will usually see directions issues specifying the service of an Appeal Skeleton Argument with the bundle of evidence relied upon by the appellant, ordinarily 28 days after the Home Office provides their bundle or 42 days after the Notice of Appeal, whichever date is later. As set out elsewhere, the Tribunal is not bound to consider only documents that were before the Secretary of State when the decision was made and any evidence relied upon that is not in the Home Office bundle should be provided for the Tribunal to consider. Following service of the bundle and ASA, a review by the Home Office should follow. If the decision is maintained, the Tribunal will list the case for a hearing.

Deadlines To Appeal

Appeals brought from within the UK have to be made within14 days from the date the decision was sent. An appeal from outside of the UK has to be brought within 28 days from the date the decision was sent. Late appeals must explain why they are being made out of time and the Tribunal will decide if it can still hear the appeal.

Documents To Be Aware Of:

(i) Procedure Rules of the First-tier Tribunal Immigration and Asylum Chamber

(ii) Presidential Guidance and Practice Statements of the First-tier Tribunal Immigration and Asylum Chamber

CHAPTER TEN

BEGUM, NATIONAL SECURITY AND APPEALS AGAINST SECTION 40(2) DECISIONS

The case of Shamima Begum has received widespread publicity in the UK due to the age she left the UK, the circumstances around her exit, her time and activities in Syria and the decision by the Secretary of State to deprive her of her British citizenship. There have been various legal challenges to decisions taken by the Secretary of State in respect of Ms. Begum including the decision to deprive her of her British citizenship.

Shamima Begum

Shamima Begum was born in the UK and was a British citizen from birth. In February 2015, at the age of 15, she left the UK with two of her schoolfriends and travelled to Syria, where she joined up with the terror group Islamic State of Iraq and the Levant (ISIL). In February 2019, she was located in the Al-Hawl refugee camp in Northern Syria.

On 19 February 2019, the Secretary of State notified Shamima Begum that he intended to deprive her of her British citizenship under section 40(2). The notice stated the reason for the decision was that she is "*a British/Bangladeshi dual national who it is assessed has previously travelled to Syria and aligned with ISIL*", and that "*[i]t is assessed that [her] return to the UK would present a risk to the national security of the [UK].*" The decision was certified under section 40A(2) in that the decision had been taken partly in reliance on information which, in the Secretary of State's opinion, should not be made public both in the interest of national security and also the public interest.

Shamima Begum sought leave to enter the UK outside of the Immigration Rules, which was refused. She appealed that decision so far as it was concerned with her human rights claim and since there was no general right of appeal to SIAC in respect of that decision, also challenged the decision to refuse entry in the Administrative Court by means of an application for judicial review. She also appealed the decision to deprive her of her British citizenship. The appeals and a rolled-up hearing for judicial review were heard concurrently by SIAC. An appeal against the decision of SIAC was heard in the Court of Appeal.

Supreme Court Decision

The cases ended up in the Supreme Court in **R (Begum) v Special Immigration Appeals Commission**[27]. The Court determined that whilst section 2B of the Special Immigration Appeals Act 1997 provides for an appeal rather than a review, the approach that should be taken is on essentially the same principles that apply in administrative law, save that it is obliged to determine for itself whether the decision was compatible with the obligations of the decision-maker under the Human Rights Act 1998. The reasons for that conclusion are set out by the Court in paragraphs 66 to 71 of the judgment.

At paragraph 118-119 of the decision the Court set out that:

> *"118. Turning next to the appeal against the deprivation decision, under section 2B of the 1997 Act, I have explained at paras 66-71 above why I respectfully disagree with the view that SIAC's jurisdiction places it "in the shoes" of the Secretary of State and entitles it to exercise de novo the discretion conferred on him by section 40(2) of the 1981 Act in the light of the evidence before it.*

---

27 [2021] UKSC 7

> *119. The scope of SIAC's jurisdiction in an appeal against a decision taken under section 40(2) was summarised in para 71 above: first, to determine whether the Secretary of State has acted in a way in which no reasonable Secretary of State could have acted, or has taken into account some irrelevant matter, or has disregarded something to which he should have given weight, or has been guilty of some procedural impropriety; secondly, to determine whether he has erred in law, for example by making findings of fact which are unsupported by any evidence or are based upon a view of the evidence which could not reasonably be held; thirdly, to determine whether he has complied with section 40(4); and fourthly, to determine whether he has acted in breach of any other legal principles applicable to his decision, such as the obligation arising in appropriate cases under section 6 of the Human Rights Act.*

Approach to Appeals

The following important points can be taken from the decision in **Begum:**

(i) Section 40(2) of the BNA 1981, empowers the Secretary of State, not SIAC, to decide whether it is "conducive to the public good" to deprive a person of their British citizenship.

(ii) Parliament did not intend to confer a discretion on SIAC.

(iii) Section 2B of the SIAC Act, provides for a right of appeal against (and not merely a right to seek review of) deprivation decisions.

(iv) The characterisation of a jurisdiction as appellate does not determine the principles of law which the appellate body must apply. The jurisdiction may have different aspects to which different principles apply.

(v) In appeals under section 2B of the SIAC Act, the principles to be applied by SIAC in reviewing the Secretary of State's exercise of discretion are largely the same as those applicable in judicial review.

(vi) If the question arises whether Secretary of State has acted incompatibly with ECHR rights, contrary to section 6 of the Human Rights Act 1998 ("HRA"), SIAC must answer that question objectively, on the basis of its own assessment.

(vii) The exercise of the discretion conferred by section 40(2) may involve consideration of national security and public safety.

(viii) Some aspects of Secretary of State's national security assessment are not justiciable. Others will depend on an evaluative judgment of matters which are incapable of objectively verifiable assessment. In relation to matters of this kind, appropriate respect should be accorded by SIAC to Secretary of State's assessment, for reasons of institutional capacity and democratic accountability.

(ix) On a human rights appeal, it is for SIAC to decide for itself, giving the appropriate weight to the Home Secretary's assessment, whether the decision constituted a disproportionate interference with an individual's ECHR rights.

Following the Supreme Court's judgment, the function of SIAC in considering appeals under section 40(2) as outlined at paragraph 71 of the judgment are:

1. Assessing whether the Secretary of State has acted in a way in which no reasonable Secretary of State could have acted, or has taken into account some irrelevant matter, or has disregarded something to which he should have given weight, or has been guilty of some procedural impropriety;

2. Considering whether the Secretary of State has erred in law, for example by making findings of fact which are unsupported by any evidence or are based upon a view of the evidence which could not reasonably be held;

3. Determining whether the Secretary of State complied with section 40(4); and

4. Considering whether the Secretary of State has acted in breach of any other legal principles applicable to his decision, such as the obligation arising in appropriate cases under section 6 of the Human Rights Act.

As such, although an appeal, the scope of the applicable jurisdiction is limited. It is not the role of SIAC to come to its own view on the case and substitute it for that of the Secretary of State's. The limitation is perhaps helpfully illustrated by a further hearing involving Shamima Begum. Following the Supreme Court's judgment, a further appeal was heard by SIAC between 21 and 25 November 2022 with the judgment being handed down on 22 February 2023.

Begum V SSHD 2023 SIAC Judgment

In her appeal to SIAC following the ruling by the Supreme Court, Shamima Begum argued that the Secretary of State had failed to take into account a relevant consideration, namely that she may have been trafficked to Syria as a child in 2015. She also argued that the Secretary of State had failed to apply their own policy. She also argued that the deprivation decision failed to respect her human rights under Article 4 of the European Convention on Human Rights because there was, at the very least, a credible suspicion that she was the victim of trafficking.

The appeal was dismissed. SIAC reiterated that following the decision in the Supreme Court it must apply administrative law principles and cannot substitute its own view on matters for that of the Secretary of

State. SIAC said the Supreme Court had made the scope of appeals very clear in its judgment in Ms Begum's case. As such, its role is confined to an examination of whether there was a proper basis in fact and in law for the Secretary of State's decision, applying well established principles to that exercise.

SIAC noted that if asked to evaluate all the circumstances of Ms Begum's case, reasonable people with knowledge of all the relevant evidence would differ, in particular in relation to the issue of the extent to which her travel to Syria was voluntary and the weight to be given to that factor in the context of all others. Likewise, it noted, reasonable people will differ as to the threat she posed in February 2019 to the national security of the United Kingdom, and as to how that threat should be balanced against all countervailing considerations. Given the remit of appeals to SIAC, against decisions under Section 40 of the BNA 1981 those sensitive issues are for the Secretary of State to evaluate and not for the Commission. The question for SIAC was whether the Secretary of State, on advice, came to a conclusion which was reasonably open to him in the light of all the available evidence, which SIAC concluded he had.

Supreme Court Decision in Begum on Approach to Appeals

Following the Supreme Court decision in Begum the approach that should be taken in appeals against a decision to deprive under section 40(2) is on, essentially the same principles that apply in administrative law, save that it is obliged to determine for itself whether the decision was compatible with the obligations of the decision-maker under the Human Rights Act 1998. The appellate court is not to substitute its discretion for that of the Secretary of State. Individuals will therefore have a harder task in succeeding on appeals, given the scope of considerations for Courts under section 40A appeals.

In **Secretary of State for the Home Department v P3**[28] in a postscript to her judgment Laing LJ identified some concerns with too narrow of an approach being taken by SIAC on cases following the decision in Begum. At paragraph 115 Laing LJ clarified:

> *"…On the appeals which are not statutory reviews, SIAC is not confined, on all issues which might arise on that appeal, to applying public law principles, still less to considering only the materials which were before the Secretary of State when the Secretary of State made the impugned decision."*

Laing LJ outlined two relevant distinctions in approaches:

(i) On some issues, the law does not require SIAC to apply a traditional public law approach at all (for example, on issues about Convention rights); and

(ii) Even where SIAC is limited to applying public law principles, it does not necessarily follow that SIAC should confine itself to material which was before the Secretary of State.

In terms of the later of the two, Laing LJ explained that SIAC is entitled to take into account material which comes to light and might not have been before the Secretary of State when she made the decision. Also, that SIAC may exclude material which the Secretary of State took into account, for example, if it decides that there is a risk that it was obtained as a result of Article 3 ill treatment. Laing LJ stated that when SIAC hears evidence on an appeal, which was not before the Secretary of State, it is entitled to make of that evidence what it may.

[28] [2021] EWCA Civ 1642 (08 November 2021)

What About Appeals Against Section 40(3) Decisions or Not Involving Issues of National Security?

A question arising following **Begum** is whether the same approach should be taken by Courts in respect of decision to deprive that don't involve national security issues and the decision to deprive was taken under section 40(3).

CHAPTER ELEVEN

FIRST-TIER TRIBUNAL (IAC) / SECTION 40(3) APPEALS POST BEGUM

The Supreme Court judgment in **Begum** was considering an appeal under section 40(2) of the British Nationality Act 1981 'the BNA 1981' that had been certified by the Secretary of State under section 40A(2). Does the same limited approach to appeals apply to appeals to the First-Tier Tribunal or in respect of decision to deprive under section 40(3) of the BNA 1981? That question is seemingly yet to be fully resolved.

There are at least two appeals underway in the Court of Appeal[29] which concern the correctness of what was said in **Ciceri v Secretary of State for the Home Department**[30] and the application of what was said in **Begum** to an appeal under s40(3) of the BNA 1981 in the First-Tier Tribunal. The Upper Tribunal (IAC) has sought to grapple with the issue, first in **Ciceri** and most recently in **Chimi (deprivation appeals, scope and evidence)**[31].

[29] Permission was granted by Newey LJ on 24 November 2022 in Ahmed v SSHD (CA/2022/001854)

[30] [2021] UKUT 238 (IAC); [2021] Imm AR 1909

[31] [2023] UKUT 00115

Ciceri v Secretary of State for the Home Department

The Upper Tribunal had seemingly answered the question of what approach should be taken in **Ciceri**. In **Ciceri**, the President held that the legal principles regarding appeals under section 40A were as follows:

> *"Following KV (Sri Lanka) v Secretary of State for the Home Department [2018] EWCA Civ 2483, Aziz v Secretary of State for the Home Department [2018] EWCA Civ 1884, Hysaj (deprivation of citizenship: delay) [2020] UKUT 128 (IAC), R (Begum) v Special Immigration Appeals Commission [2021] UKSC 7 and Laci v Secretary of State for the Home Department [2021] EWCA Civ 769 the legal principles regarding appeals under section 40A of the British Nationality Act 1981 against decisions to deprive a person of British citizenship are as follows:*
>
>> *1) The Tribunal must first establish whether the relevant condition precedent specified in section 40(2) or (3) of the British Nationality Act 1981 exists for the exercise of the discretion whether to deprive the appellant of British citizenship. In a section 40(3) case, this requires the Tribunal to establish whether citizenship was obtained by one or more of the means specified in that subsection. In answering the condition precedent question, the Tribunal must adopt the approach set out in paragraph 71 of the judgment in Begum, which is to consider whether the Secretary of State has made findings of fact which are unsupported by any evidence or are based on a view of the evidence that could not reasonably be held.*
>>
>> …"

The Upper Tribunal set out that the principles outlined in **Begum** were equally applicable to decisions made under section 40(3). As such the guidance given in **Ciceri** was that appeals to the First-Tier Tribunal and against decisions under section 40(3) are limited to the same public law arguments as outlined at paragraph 71 of the Supreme Court's decision in **Begum**. The Upper Tribunal in **Ciceri**, however, did not provide a specific explanation as to why the principles outlined in Begum were equally applicable to a decision made under section 40(3). Indeed, the specific question being considered by the Upper Tribunal was Article 8, rather than the scope of an appeal under section 40A of the BNA 1981. The Court of Appeal refused permission to appeal in **Ciceri** on 4th May 2022, Lewis LJ in doing so pointed out that the appellant had effectively conceded his fraud.

Is it arguable that the Tribunal is not bound by the approach in Begum?

A number of arguments have been made in the First-Tier Tribunal and Upper Tribunal that **Ciceri** should not be followed, in order that the Tribunal can make its own findings of fact on the evidence, rather than being limited to administrative law arguments. That approach would offer appellant's a wider scope to argue that the decision taken was incorrect.

Although pre-dating the decision in Begum, in **Pirzada (Deprivation of citizenship: general principles)**[32]**,** the Upper Tribunal set out a similar approach in that:

> *"The restrictions on the rights of appeal imposed by s 84 of the 2002 Act do not apply to appeals against a s 40 decision: therefore, any proper ground of appeal is available to an applicant. The grounds of appeal are, however, limited by the formulation of s 40 and must be directed to whether the Secretary of State's decision was in fact empowered by that section. There is no suggestion that a Tribunal has the power to consider whether it is satisfied of any of the matters set out in*

[32] [2017] UKUT 196 (IAC)

> *sub-ss (2) or (3); nor is there any suggestion that the Tribunal can itself exercise the Secretary of State's discretion."*

In **BA (deprivation of citizenship: appeals)**[33] the Upper Tribunal observed that there were problems with those findings in **Pirzada**. It noted that the Tribunal in **Pirzada** had not been referred to the decision in **Arusha and Demushi (deprivation of citizenship – delay)**[34] nor the decision in **Deliallisi (British Citizen: deprivation appeal; Scope)**[35]. The Upper Tribunal in BA held that the passage in paragraph 9E of **Pirzada** (set out above) should not be followed.

Leggatt LJ in **KV (Sri Lanka) v Secretary of State for the Home Department**[36] at paragraph 6 of his judgment (with which Sir Geoffrey Vos C and Haddon-Cave LJ agreed) set out a summary of the principles applicable in an appeal under section 40A, as follows:

> *"The task of the tribunal on such an appeal has been considered by the Upper Tribunal (Immigration and Asylum Chamber) in a number of cases including **Deliallisi (British Citizen: deprivation appeal; Scope) [2013] UKUT 439 (IAC)** and, more recently, **BA (deprivation of citizenship: Appeals) [2018] UKUT 85 (IAC)**. I would endorse the following principles which are articulated in those decisions and which I did not understand to be in dispute on this appeal:*
>
> > *(1) Like an appeal under section 82 of the Nationality, Immigration and Asylum Act 2002, an appeal under section 40A of the 1981 Act is not a review of the Secretary of State's decision but a full reconsideration*

33 [2018] UKUT 85 (IAC)

34 [2012] UKUT 80(IAC)

35 [2013] UKUT 439 (IAC)

36 [2018] EWCA Civ 2483, [2018] 4 WLR 166

> *of the decision whether to deprive the appellant of British citizenship.*
>
> *(2) It is thus for the tribunal to find the relevant facts on the basis of the evidence adduced to the tribunal, whether or not that evidence was before the Secretary of State when deciding to make a deprivation order.*
>
> *(3) The tribunal must first establish whether the relevant condition precedent specified in section 40 (2) or (3) exists for the exercise of the discretion whether to deprive the appellant of British citizenship. In a section 40 (3) case, this requires the tribunal to establish whether citizenship was obtained by one or more of the means specified in that subsection.*
>
> *(4) If the condition precedent is established, the tribunal has then to ask whether the Secretary of State's discretion to deprive the appellant of British citizenship should be exercised differently. For this purpose, the tribunal must first determine the reasonably foreseeable consequences of deprivation.*
>
> *(5) If the rights of the appellant or any other relevant person under article 8 of the European Convention on Human Rights are engaged, the tribunal will have to decide whether depriving the appellant of British citizenship would constitute a disproportionate interference with those rights. But even if article 8 is not engaged, the tribunal must still consider whether the discretion should be exercised differently."*

The approach to be taken in an appeal under section 40A as set out by the Court in **<u>KV</u>** was that it "*is not a review of the Secretary of State's decision but a full reconsideration of the decision whether to deprive the appellant of British citizenship.*" The Court of Appeal's decision in **<u>KV</u>**

does not appear to have been referred to the Supreme Court in **Begum**, for its consideration. The Court of Appeal has observed on a number of occasions recently failures by representatives to draw authorities to the attention of Courts. It is important that representatives remember and comply with their duty to the Court to draw all relevant authorities to the Court's attention.

In **Laci v Secretary of State for the Home Department**[37] Underhill LJ having set out the principles in **KV** noted that they had to now be read, subject to points set out in a postscript at paragraph 40 of his judgment in **Laci**, in light of the judgment in **Begum**. At paragraph 40 of Underhill LJ's judgment, he says:

> "*Postscript. When this judgment was circulated to counsel in draft, Mr Malik drew our attention to the decision of the Supreme Court in R (Begum) v Special Immigration Appeals Commission [2021] UKSC 7, [2021] 2 WLR 556, which was handed down subsequent to the argument before us. Begum concerns a decision taken by the Secretary of State to deprive the appellant of her nationality under section 40 (2) of the 1981 Act. At paras. 32-81 of his judgment, with which the other Justices agreed, Lord Reed discusses the nature of an appeal to SIAC under section 2B of the Special Immigration Appeals Commission Act 1997, which is the equivalent of section 40A; and in that connection he discusses both Deliallisi and BA (though not KV, to which the Court does not appear to have referred). His conclusion is that while section 2B provides for an appeal rather than a review SIAC should approach its task on (to paraphrase) essentially Wednesbury principles, save that it was obliged to determine for itself whether the decision was compatible with the obligations of the decision-maker under the Human Rights Act 1998 (see para. 68). It may be that that reasoning is not confined to section 2B or to cases falling under*

[37] [2021] EWCA Civ 769 (20 May 2021)

section 40 (2), in which case some of statements quoted above about the correct approach to appeals under section 40A in the case of decisions under section 40 (3) will require qualification. But I do not think that that is something on which I should express a view here. Begum does not bear directly on the actual grounds of appeal before us, and Mr Malik made it plain that he did not wish to advance any fresh ground based on it. Rather, he was rightly concerned that we should be aware of it in the context of the more general review of the law in the preceding paragraphs. I confine myself to saying that anything said in the authorities reviewed above about the scope of an appeal under section 40A should be read subject to the decision in Begum."

Upper Tribunal Consideration of Ciceri

The Upper Tribunal considered in **Berdica v Secretary of State for the Home Department (Deprivation of citizenship: consideration)**[38] argument that the First-tier Tribunal had erred by failing to consider departing from, or distinguishing, the reported decision of **Ciceri**. The appellant advanced two complaints under this ground:

(i) the Judge erred at of her decision in concluding that the decision of **Ciceri** is 'binding authority' upon the First-tier Tribunal; and

(ii) **Ciceri** ought to have been decided differently, that the logic of Begum should properly be regarded as confined to appeals under section 40(2) of the BNA 1981, and that the correct approach in deprivation appeals under section 40(3) should remain the merits-based assessment espoused by Leggatt LJ in KV (Sri Lanka)

[38] [2022] UKUT 276 (IAC) (05 April 2022)

The Upper Tribunal concluded that the First-Tier Tribunal is bound by the decision in **Ciceri**. The Upper Tribunal noted at paragraph 43 of the determination that:

> *"As a superior court of record, the Upper Tribunal's decisions are binding on the First-tier Tribunal, not only in the individual case by virtue of section 12 [of the Tribunal, Courts and Enforcement Act 2007], but also as a matter of precedent... This is compatible with section 107(3) of the Nationality, Immigration and Asylum Act 2002 and the Practice Directions of the First-tier Tribunal and the Upper Tribunal, which provide for starred cases to be authoritative in respect of the Upper Tribunal, as well as the First-tier Tribunal."*

To emphasis the point, the headnote of **Berdica** sets out:

> *"Decisions of the Upper Tribunal are binding on the First-tier Tribunal, not only in the individual case by virtue of section 12 of the Tribunal, Courts and Enforcement Act 2007, but also as a matter of precedent."*

Court of Appeal Judgment in P3

In a postscript to the Court of Appeal's judgment in **Secretary of State for the Home Department v P3**[39] Laing LJ giving the leading judgment said at paragraph 114:

> *"Finally, in the course of his oral submissions, Mr Blundell QC indicated that SIAC might now be taking an approach to its role on appeals such as section 2B appeals which caused this Court some concern, and as I have mentioned in paragraph 6, above, led to further written submissions after the hearing. This approach seems to have been prompted by the decision in Begum.*

[39] [2021] EWCA Civ 1642 (08 November 2021)

> *I consider that this approach may be unduly narrow, and one which is not required by Begum.* ***Begum is authority for the proposition that, broadly, SIAC should take a public law approach to challenges to the Secretary of State's assessment of national security. It is not authority for any wider proposition*** *" [emphasis added]*

The paragraph may lend support to an argument that Begum is not authority that appeals under section 40(3) are limited to the public law approach as set out in paragraph 71 of **Begum** and therefore Tribunal's should instead proceed with a merits-based assessment. Does what Laing LJ say narrow the application of Begum to SIAC cases and as such supersede the Upper Tribunal's reliance on the decision in **Ciceri**? If so, it would allow a judge in the First-Tier Tribunal to consider the condition precedent question for themselves.

Against what is said in **P3** at paragraph 114, it is worth considering in the context of what is said in the following paragraph. At paragraph 115 of **P3** Laing LJ referred to situations where SIAC is not confined to apply public law principles or restricted to consider material that was before the decision maker. The first being issues concerning Convention rights. There are other examples given of when SIAC could include or exclude evidence. In **P3** Sir Stephan Irwin in his judgment at paragraph 126 referred to testing and scrutinising the evidence and Bean LJ referred at paragraph 135 to, "*proper deference [to the decision of the SSHD] in the context of properly tested evidence*".

There is therefore, arguably nothing in what was said in **P3** that supports a fact-finding role for SIAC (or the Tribunal) except when considering Convention rights. Instead, it supports the position that is necessary for the Court to consider with care the evidence that was before the decision maker in order to carry out a review of the decision on public law grounds.

The statement is paragraph 114 of **P3**, also needs to be considered in its context. The decision in P3 is confined to the specific issues before it relating to the scope of a SIAC appeal and in light of its particular procedures. The court was not considering arguments as to whether Begum might have a wider application in non-certified appeals brought in the First-tier Tribunal. As such, it appears to be a difficult argument that **P3** does undermines or supersedes what was said in **Ciceri**.

Further, the reasoning given in **Begum** by the Supreme court would appear to apply equally to decision under section 40(3) as to decisions under section 40(2). Whether an appeal against deprivation of citizenship is heard in SIAC or in the First-tier Tribunal the underlying powers to deprive a person of citizenship with reference to sections 40(2) and 40(3) are the same. The venue for the appeal, is determined by whether a certificate is issued under section 40A or not.

The Supreme Court's decision in Begum drew largely from the case of **SSHD v Rehman**[40] and the wording of the statutory provisions contained in the BNA 1981 itself. The Supreme Court emphasised that the wording of section 40(2) focussed on the exercise of discretion by the Secretary of State as illustrated by the wording 'the Secretary of State may...' (see paragraph 66 of **Begum**). The Supreme Court noted that the condition precedent was not that 'SIAC is satisfied', but that 'the Secretary of State is satisfied' that deprivation is '*conducive to the public good*' (see paragraph 67 of **Begum**). The Court then sets out in detail its reasoning for reaching the conclusion that it did at paragraph 71 of the judgment.

Perhaps importantly, similar wording is used in section 40(3), which sets out the condition precedent that 'the Secretary of State is satisfied' that naturalisation was obtained by one of the three reasons contained within the section. It would seem, that is a relevant, if not decisive, factor when considering if the same principles considered in Begum in relation to section 40(2) are also likely to apply to decisions made under section 40(3). It is certainly a point that representatives will need to grapple with

[40] [2001] UKHL 47; [2003] 1 AC 153

if seeking to rely on what is said by Laing LJ in **P3** to undermine or argue it supersedes what was said by the Upper Tribunal in **Ciceri** and **Chimi**.

Chimi

In **Chimi** the Hon. Mr Justice Dove, President of the Upper Tribunal and Upper Tribunal Judge Blundell gave consideration to the points raised in respect of **P3** and the decision of SIAC in **U3 v SSHD SC/153/2018 & SC/153/2021**, that followed **P3.** Having set out much of the law as above, the Upper Tribunal concluded that when considering an appeal under section 40A(1) of the BNA 1981 against a decision made by the respondent exercising the power under section 40(2) or 40(3) of the BNA 1981 the task of the Tribunal is to scrutinise, using established public law criteria, whether or not the conclusion that the condition precedent to depriving the appellant of citizenship has been vitiated by an error of law.

The Upper Tribunal determined that it is not the task of the Tribunal to undertake a merits-based review and redetermination of the decision on the existence of the condition precedent, as it were standing in the shoes of the respondent. It considered this to be consistent with paragraph 1 of the headnote in **Ciceri** which requires the adoption of the approach set out in paragraph 71 of the judgment in **Begum**. The Upper Tribunal[41] made clear that in paragraph 71 of Lord Reed's judgment in Begum the Court was not intending to provide an exhaustive list of the potential types of public law error which it is open to the Tribunal to conclude have affected the decision. As such other types of public law error which were not specifically identified by Lord Reed in paragraph 71 are not excluded from consideration by the Tribunal.

Having determined that the Supreme Court's decision in **Begum** must govern the analysis of the condition precedent question and the discretion question, the Upper Tribunal concluded that the structured

[41] At paragraph 56

approach set out at paragraph 6(4)-(5) of **R (KV) v SSHD** should be amended.

The headnote of **Chimi** provides for the approach to now be taken in appeals as:

> *"(1) A Tribunal determining an appeal against a decision taken by the respondent under s40(2) or s40(3) of the British Nationality Act 1981 should consider the following questions:*
>
> > *(a) Did the Secretary of State materially err in law when she decided that the condition precedent in s40(2) or s40(3) of the British Nationality Act 1981 was satisfied? If so, the appeal falls to be allowed. If not,*
> >
> > *(b) Did the Secretary of State materially err in law when she decided to exercise her discretion to deprive the appellant of British citizenship? If so, the appeal falls to be allowed. If not,*
> >
> > *(c) Weighing the lawfully determined deprivation decision against the reasonably foreseeable consequences for the appellant, is the decision unlawful under s6 of the Human Rights Act 1998? If so, the appeal falls to be allowed on human rights grounds. If not, the appeal falls to be dismissed."*

Ultimately, further guidance from the Court of Appeal or the Supreme Court on the approach to be taken by the lower Courts is likely to be forthcoming.

CHAPTER TWELVE

CONDITION PRECEDENT / DISCRETION

Following the Upper Tribunal's determination in **Chimi** the starting point for the First-Tier Tribunal on appeal is to establish whether the Secretary of State materially err in law when she decided the relevant condition precedent specified in section 40(2) or (3) of the British Nationality Act 1981 'the BNA 1981' exists. If not, the Tribunal will need to proceed to consider whether the Secretary of State materially erred when she decided to exercise her discretion to deprive the appellant of their British citizenship.

Condition precedent

Condition precedent does not mean the same as a finding of precedent fact. In a section 40(3) case, that requires the Tribunal to establish whether the appellant's British citizenship was obtained by one or more of the means specified in that subsection of the BNA 1981. In answering the condition precedent question, the Tribunal must adopt the approach set out in paragraph 71 of the Supreme Court judgment in **Begum [2021] UKSC 7**, which is to consider whether the Secretary of State has made findings of fact which are unsupported by any evidence or are based on a view of the evidence that could not reasonably be held. As noted in **Chimi** the public law grounds are not limited to those mentioned explicitly by Lord Reed in the judgment.

The Secretary of State bears the burden of proving that the appellant has deceived her. The Tribunal is required only to consider whether the Secretary of State has shown that she was entitled to reach that conclusion on the evidence.

Post-Decision Evidence

The Upper Tribunal in **Berdica (Deprivation of citizenship: consideration)**[42] concluded that in deprivation of citizenship appeals, consideration is to be given both to the sustainability of the original decision and also whether upon considering subsequent evidence the Secretary of State's maintenance of her decision up to and including the hearing is also sustainable. However, the Upper Tribunal confirmed recently in **Chimi** that in considering the first two questions in an appeal the Tribunal must only consider evidence which was before the Secretary of State or which is otherwise relevant to establishing a pleaded error of law in the decision under challenge. The Upper Tribunal made clear that **Berdica** should not be followed with respect to what was said about new evidence.

Sleiman [2017] UKUT 367 (IAC)

Cases arising from leave being granted during the 'legacy process' occur frequently. The Upper Tribunal's decision in **Sleiman (deprivation of citizenship; conduct: Lebanon)**[43] is discussed in chapter 5 of this book and involved an individual. It is important to note that in terms of 'condition precedent' that there were limited submissions made by the Secretary of State in the appeal. That was due to a concession made in the appeal that the Secretary of State had recognised during the legacy review that the appellant had given two different dates of birth but had stated in terms in an internal note that the appellant's age was irrelevant to the decision to grant. Owing to the concession there was no review of authorities relating to the question of how legacy reviews were conducted and what was or was not considered by caseworkers in that context

42 [2022] UKUT 00276 (IAC)

43 [2017] UKUT 367 (IAC) (19 July 2017)

In considering cases where the issues in **Sleiman** may arise, it may assist to have regard to the decision judgment of Burton J in **Hakemi & Ors v SSHD**[44]. Burton J drew attention to the methodology of reviews in "legacy" cases at paragraphs 6 and 7 of the judgment, and draws particular attention to the guidance which underlay reviews of legacy cases (Chapter 53 of the Enforcement Instructions and Guidance) and the need to consider factors relating to a person's personal history which might outweigh other considerations.

A further consideration is what was said by Upper Tribunal Judge Kopieczek at paragraph 62 of the decision in Sleiman, that the respondent could have, but did not, pursue an argument that the lie as to age impacted on the grant of citizenship based on the fact that the appellant was not entitled to the leave he had wrongfully obtained as a minor. Continuation of the false identity may well be relevant even where leave was granted through the 'legacy' process. The question is not whether the individual obtained ILR by fraud, but whether they obtained naturalisation by fraud, false representation or concealment of a material fact. Not being open about the utilisation of a false identity can be relevant, particular in respect of the '*good character*' requirement when naturalising.

The current Home Office Guidance, 'Guide AN, Naturalisation Booklet, The Requirements and The Process'[45] provides:

> "You must say whether you have been involved in anything which might indicate that you are not of good character. You must give information about any of these activities no matter how long ago it was. Checks will be made in all cases and your application may fail and your fee will not be refunded if you make an untruthful declaration. If you are in any doubt about whether you have done something, or it has

---

[44] [2012] EWHC 1967 (Admin)

[45] Published October 2022

> been alleged that you have done something, which might lead us to think that you are not of good character, you should say so."

Under the heading '*deception*', the guidance states:

> "You must tell us if you have practised deception in your dealings with the Home Office or other government departments (for example, by providing false information or fraudulent documents)."

Similar wording has appeared in previous versions of the guidance. It is important therefore to bear in mind when advising individuals that are seeking to naturalise of the consequences of using deception or maintaining identities or details which are false and implication of that guidance in respect of decisions that might be made under section 40(3) of the BNA 1981.

What Happens if the Secretary of State Materially Errs in Law When She Decided That the Condition Precedent in S40(2) Or S40(3) Of the British Nationality Act 1981 Was Satisfied?

If the Secretary of State materially erred in deciding the condition precedent, the appeal falls to be allowed. If not, the Tribunal must proceed to determine whether the Secretary of State materially err in law when she decided to exercise her discretion to deprive the appellant of British citizenship. If she did, the appeal falls to be allowed. If not, the Tribunal must proceed to determine whether the rights of the appellant or any other relevant person under the ECHR are engaged; usually ECHR Article 8.

CHAPTER THIRTEEN

ECHR

If the Tribunal reaches this stage, it must proceed to determine whether the rights of the appellant or any other relevant person under the ECHR are engaged. Usually that will be Article 8 of the ECHR (Right to a family / private life). If they are engaged, the Tribunal will then need to consider whether depriving the appellant of his British citizenship would violate his rights, contrary to the obligation under section 6 of the Human Rights Act 1998 for the Secretary of State not to act in a way that is incompatible with the ECHR.

Article 8

Article 8 the right to respect for private and family life provides that:

> *"1. Everyone has the right to respect for his private and family life, his home and his correspondence.*
>
> *2. There shall be no interference by a public authority with the exercise of this right except such as is in accordance with the law and is necessary in a democratic society in the interests of national security, public safety or the economic well-being of the country, for the prevention of disorder or crime, for the protection of health or morals, or for the protection of the rights and freedoms of others."*

Approach for the Tribunal to Take

In **Chimi** the Upper Tribunal set out that the Tribunal must weigh the lawfully determined deprivation decision against the reasonably foreseeable consequences for the appellant, in order to determine whether the decision is unlawful under s6 of the Human Rights Act 1998. If it is, the appeal falls to be allowed on human rights grounds. If not, the appeal falls to be dismissed.

In **Ciceri** the Tribunal set out that in considering whether the decision would violate the appellant's ECHR rights the Tribunal must determine the reasonably foreseeable consequences of deprivation; but it will not be necessary or appropriate for the Tribunal, at least usually, to conduct a proleptic assessment of the likelihood of the appellant being lawfully removed from the United Kingdom.

In **Aziz v Secretary of State for the Home Department**[46], Sales LJ held that "*at least in the usual case*" it was "*neither necessary nor appropriate for a tribunal considering the deprivation question to conduct a 'proleptic assessment' of the likelihood of a lawful removal*" (see paragraph 26 of judgment). To that extent, therefore, the determination of the reasonably foreseeable consequences of deprivation must, usually, exclude the issue of removal.

The Upper Tribunal in **Muslija (deprivation: reasonably foreseeable consequences)**[47] provided some useful guidance on the approach to be taken. The Upper Tribunal observed that as the reasonably foreseeable consequences of the deprivation of citizenship are relevant to an assessment of the proportionality of the decision, for Article 8(2) ECHR purposes, and as the Tribunal must conduct that assessment for itself, it is necessary for the Tribunal to determine the reasonably foreseeable consequences for itself.

The Upper Tribunal considered it to be highly unlikely that a Tribunal's assessment of the reasonably foreseeable consequences of a deprivation order could legitimately be extended to prospective future decisions of the Secretary of State in relate to the appellant, following the loss of the

46 [2018] EWCA Civ 1884; [2019] Imm AR 264

47 [2022] UKUT 337 (IAC) (16 November 2022)

right of abode. The Tribunal also concluded that exposure to the "limbo period", between the decision to deprive and consideration of a grant of alternative leave, without more, could not possibly tip the proportionality balance in favour of an appellant retaining British citizenship they had obtained fraudulently. The Upper Tribunal considered there would be limits to the "utility of an assessment of the length of the limbo period; in the absence of some other factor" and that the mere fact of exposure to even a "potentially lengthy period of limbo" is a factor unlikely to be of dispositive relevance.

The Upper Tribunal emphasised the difference between the consequence decision to deprive an individual of their British citizenship and a future Human Rights claim in respect of removal. The Upper Tribunal cautioned that *"an overly anticipatory analysis of the reasonably foreseeable consequences of deprivation will be founded on speculation"*.

New evidence

In considering matters relating to the ECHR the Tribunal is entitled to consider evidence which was not before the Secretary of State but, in doing so, it may not use the new evidence to revisit the questions of whether there was a material error in respect of the condition precedent or the exercise of the Secretary of State's discretion.

Proportionality

Any relevant assessment of proportionality is for the Tribunal to make, on the evidence before it. The evidence need not be the same as the evidence considered by the Secretary of State. As such the appellant may rely on evidence post-dating the decision to deprive them of their British citizenship in establishing why the decision to deprive them is a disproportionate outcome.

In determining proportionality, the Tribunal must pay due regard to the "inherent weight that will normally lie on the Secretary of State's side of the scales in the Article 8 balancing exercise", given the importance of maintaining the integrity of British nationality law in the face of attempts by individuals to subvert it particularly in section 40(3) case where there is fraudulent conduct.

The proportionality balancing exercise in Article 8(2) will involve the exercise of judicial discretion, it is a mixed question of fact and law leading to the making of a value judgment.

The Upper Tribunal in **Hysaj (Deprivation of Citizenship: Delay)**[48] recorded in the headnote that:

> *"There is a heavy weight to be placed upon the public interest in maintaining the integrity of the system by which foreign nationals are naturalised and permitted to enjoy the benefits of British citizenship. Any effect on day-to-day life that may result from a person being deprived of British citizenship is a consequence of the that person's fraud or deception and, without more, cannot tip the proportionality balance, so as to compel the respondent to grant a period of leave, whether short or otherwise."*

This was endorsed in **Laci v Secretary of State for the Home Department**[49] by Underhill LJ at paragraph 80 of the judgment.

---

48 [2020] UKUT 128 (IAC)

49 [2021] EWCA Civ 769 (20 May 2021)

Delay

Any delay by the Secretary of State in making a decision under section 40(2) or (3) may be relevant to the question of whether the decision amounts to a disproportionate interference with Article 8. Lord Bingham in **EB (Kosovo) v Secretary of State for the Home Department**[50], recognised that delay on the part of the respondent in reaching a decision in an individual's case can affect the outcome of an appeal on the ground that removal would violate Article 8. Lord Bingham at paragraphs 13 to 16 of the judgment identified three ways in which it could do so:

> *"(1) The longer an applicant remains in the country the more likely they are to develop close personal and social ties and put down roots of a kind which deserve protection under Article 8;*
>
> *(2) The more time goes by without any steps being taken to remove an applicant, the more the sense of impermanence which will imbue relationships formed earlier in the period will fade "and the expectation will grow that if the authorities had intended to remove the applicant they would have taken steps to do so", which may affect the proportionality of removal.*
>
> *(3) Delay may "reduce the weight otherwise to be accorded to the requirements of firm and fair immigration control, if the delay is shown to be the result of a dysfunctional system which yields unpredictable, inconsistent and unfair outcomes"."*

In **Hysaj (Deprivation of Citizenship: Delay)** the Upper Tribunal considered amongst other issues the question of delay in seeking to deprive an individual of their British citizenship, because the Secretary of State had erroneously sought to declare their citizenship a nullity[51]. The Upper Tribunal concluded that any period during which the Secretary of

[50] [2009] AC 1159

[51] See Chapter 16 on nullity

State was adopting the (mistaken) stance that the grant of citizenship to the appellant was a nullity will not normally be relevant in assessing the effects of delay by reference to the second and third of Lord Bingham's points in **EB (Kosovo)**.

In **Laci** Underhill LJ at paragraph 78 distinguished between the type of delay in Hysaj; which arose from the respondent's decision to pursue the "nullity" route, and, as in Laci, delay that, upon analysis, could not properly be attributed to the issue of nullity. He held that "where there is something more (as, here, the Secretary of State's prolonged and unexplained delay/inaction), the problems that may arise in the limbo period may properly carry weight in the overall assessment". As such inaction on the part of the Secretary of State resulting in delay maybe considered as being sufficiently compelling, when taken with the other circumstances of a case, to justify a decision that the appellant should not be deprived of his citizenship".

What If the Decision Does Not Breach The ECHR?

If the Tribunal concludes that the decision does not breach the ECHR, the appeal falls to be dismissed.

CHAPTER FOURTEEN

CONSEQUENCES

A decision to deprive an individual of their British citizenship results in that individual losing their British nationality and usually with it the right of abode. The individual will not resort back to any previous immigration status they may have held. Any appeal against the decision under section 40A of the British Nationality Act or section 2B of Special Immigration Appeals Commission Act 1997 are non-suspensive.

Out of the UK

Being out of the UK does not prevent deprivation from taking place, the loss of the right of abode without the reinstatement of any previous immigration status means an individual would need to seek Entry Clearance in order to return to the UK to participate in proceedings (see for example **Begum**).

The question as to whether an individual should be grated Entry Clearance to participate in proceedings, is separate from the decision to deprive. Factors leading to the decision to deprive are, however, likely to be relevant.

At paragraphs 85-87 of **R (W2 and IA) v Secretary of State for the Home Department**[52] the Court of Appeal made '*it clear that the issue for the Commission on a case such as this is whether an out-of-country appeal would be effective*'. If SIAC '*were to conclude that an appellant's presence in this country is necessary in order for his appeal to be effective, it will allow the appeal against refusal [of leave to enter] (paragraph 85)*'

[52] [2017] EWCA Civ 2146 (19 December 2017)

The Court of Appeal concluded:

> *"...there is no reason why SIAC, in the course of a section 2 appeal of a refusal of LTE [Leave to Enter], could not determine and give a practical and effective remedy to the question whether it is necessary for W2 to be in the country for his appeal to be effective and to do so before the hearing of the substantive appeal. This could be done by hearing the appeal against a decision to refuse W2 LTE if, as seems likely to be the case, the Secretary of State will so decide, together with its consideration of this issue as a preliminary issue in the appeal."*

Removal?

A decision to deprive an individual of their British citizenship is not a decision to remove them from the UK. A subsequent decision will often follow, considering whether or not the individual should also be removed in the UK. At that time consideration to matters not relevant to the deprivation decision can be taken into account; for example, would removal of the individual breach Article 8 of the ECHR due to his family or private life. This is distinct from whether deprivation would breach Article 8[53].

Withdrawal Of Decision

In **E3 & Ors v Secretary of State for the Home Department**[54] the Court of appeal considered whether the withdraw of a deprivation order, following the Secretary of State accepting that the decision made the individuals stateless, means that it should be treated as if it had never been made and never had legal effect, so that the person is to be treated

---

53 See Chapter 13

54 [2023] EWCA Civ 26 (17 January 2023)

as someone who was at all times a British citizen? Or does the withdrawal only take effect from the date that the order was withdrawn?

At paragraph 50 of the judgment, the Court of Appeal concluded that the withdrawal of the deprivation orders in the appellants' cases took effect on the date that they were withdrawn. Further, the statutory scheme, with the possibility of appealing to SIAC on the question of whether a decision to make a deprivation order has the result of rendering a person stateless, does not have the effect that any deprivation order which is withdrawn is to be regarded as unlawful or a nullity, that is, as incapable of having produced legal effects in the past

The decision means that individuals whose British citizenship is withdrawn are not British citizen from the date of the order, even if the order is subsequently withdrawn by the Secretary of State. As such any children born to an individual during that period would not be able to acquire British citizenship from the individual.

Success On Appeal

A successful appeal establishing that an individual would be made stateless by a decision to deprive them under section 40(2) of the BNA 1981 results in that deprivation being unlawful by virtue of section 40(4) (subject to section 40(4A)).

Given the scope of appeals post **Begum** and **Chimi**, the consequence of succeeding does not emphatically mean that the individual cannot be deprived of their British citizenship, as it will be for the Secretary of State to consider whether to initiate a further deprivation process, to address the deficiencies identified by the Court.

CHAPTER FIFTEEN

NULLITY

The Home Office's Nullity of British citizenship guidance version 1.0 'the guidance' was published on 10 May 2023. It replaced the longstanding and out of date Home Office caseworker guidance. The new guidance provides clarification on the use of nullity following the Supreme Court's judgment in **Hysaj and Bakijasi**[55].

The guidance confirms that the test for whether a registration or naturalisation was a nullity has been developed through case law and so is not directly provided for in the British nationality legislation. If the grant of citizenship is a nullity, deprivation under the British Nationality Act 1981 is not required.

There are two circumstances in which a decision to grant an individual British citizenship following an application for registration or naturalisation may be a nullity. They are:

(i) If it is discovered that the applicant is not the intended recipient of the grant; or

(ii) The applicant already has the status

If either of the above circumstances are considered to apply, the Secretary of State need only be satisfied that the citizenship registration or naturalisation was not technically obtained in law for the naturalisation or registration to be considered a nullity. The consequence of the grant of citizenship being a nullity is the registration or naturalisation is deemed not to have ever taken place. The grant having been ineffective from the outset means the individual will never have been a British citizen

[55] R (Hysaj & Ors) v SSHD [2017] UKSC 82

and this therefore may have consequences not just for the individual but for their family members as well.

The applicant is not the intended recipient of the grant

In **Hysaj & Ors**, the Supreme Court addressed the question of when a declaration of nullity rather than deprivation was the appropriate course for the Secretary of State to follow. The Court confirmed the limits of the use of declarations of nullity by the Secretary of State.

The issue before the court in **Hysaj** was whether the misrepresentations made by the appellants in their applications for citizenship made the grant of that citizenship a nullity, rather than rendering them liable to be deprived of that citizenship under sections 40 and 40A of the British Nationality Act 1981. The judgment was given in unusual circumstances as the Court allowed the case by consent.

Although, the outcome of the appeal was settled by consent, the Supreme Court considered four earlier decisions of the Court of Appeal in relation to nullity decisions:

(i) R v Secretary of State for the Home Department, Ex p Sultan Mahmood [1981] QB 58

(ii) R v Secretary of State for the Hone Department, Ex p Parvaz Akhtar [1981] QB 46

(iii) R v Secretary of State for the Home Department, Ex p Ejaz [1994] QB 496

(iv) Bibi v Entry Clearance Officer, Dhaka [2007] EWCA Civ 740, [2008] INLR 683

The Supreme Court agreed with the Secretary of State that there had been "*a gradual expansion of the nullity approach since **Mahmood***". Although, **Mahmood** and **Ejaz** had been rightly decided, the Court accepted the SSHD's position the law had taken a wrong turn after **Mahmood** and the Court of Appeal decisions in **Akhtar** and **Bibi** were wrongly decided.

Mahmood had involved two real people, X and Y. X had impersonated Y for the purpose of applying for citizenship. Y had the characteristics required for citizenship. Y was considered for naturalisation by the Secretary of State and was granted citizenship. But Y had never applied to become a British citizenship, may not have wanted it, or may even have been dead. Accordingly, it could not be said that citizenship had been granted either to Y or to X and there was therefore no grant of citizenship. The Court held that deprivation was not required as the grant was a nullity.

In contrast, the later cases, involved individuals using a false identity created by them or on their behalf, and it was in that identity they acquire the characteristics needed to obtain citizenship. The Court in **Hysaj** summarised the position as, "X applies for citizenship using the false identity Y. But X meets the requirements for citizenship albeit having acquired them by using the false identity Y. X is considered for citizenship by the Secretary of State in identity Y and is granted citizenship in that identity." It was accepted that in those circumstance the grant of citizenship is valid. As such the SSHD would need to go through the deprivation provisions under section 40.

The Supreme Court therefore confirmed that where a person applies for citizenship in the identity of another person, who 'has never applied for it, may not want it, or may even be dead', the naturalisation or registration will be a nullity. Where, however, a person meets the requirements for citizenship in a false identity, for example by falsifying their name, nationality, date or place of birth, deprivation is the appropriate course.

The updated Home Office guidance confirms the test for caseworkers to apply in considering the issue of nullity, is the approach as set out in

Hysaj. The guidance gives helpful examples of when cases would not be a nullity including:

- X adopts the identity of Y, where Y is a false identity created by X, and Y has the characteristics required for citizenship
- X adopts the identity of Y, where Y is a real person, and in adopting the identity of Y, X acquires the characteristics required for citizenship
- X adopts the identity of Y, where Y is a false identity created by X, and in adopting the identity of Y, X acquires the characteristics required for citizenship

The guidance sets out that in order to determine if a grant of citizenship is a nullity, the decision maker must decide whether there is wholesale impersonation of another real person or if there are merely fictitious elements of the identity. This requires carefully consideration as to whether the person has merely falsified some of their own details or has assumed the complete identity of another person. The guidance notes that in cases where there is an element of fictitious identity, that is a person has falsified some of their own details, but not wholesale impersonation it would not be nullity cases. Such cases would be considered instead for deprivation on the grounds of fraud under section 40(3)[56].

Already has status

Where somebody already has citizenship, an application for registration or naturalisation will usually be treated as a nullity. As the Secretary of State observes in the guidance such an application would add nothing to the status the individual already enjoys and at best offers no more than

56 British Nationality Act 1981

confirmation of their status as a British citizen. An individual is not able to hold two lots of British citizenship.

Circumstances which may lead to nullity under this heading include where an individual was unaware that they were British by birth, having been born in the UK but left as a child, and later applies to naturalise or register as a British citizen. Such an application would be unnecessary as they are already a British citizen. In those circumstances, the application will usually be treated as a nullity and the application fee refunded. The guidance states, "usually" but doesn't identify any circumstances in which an application qualifying under this head would not be treated as null and void. Indeed, it is difficult to envisage a scenario where a subsequent application by somebody who was already a British citizen would not be treated as null and void.

In order to minimise potential errors, caseworkers at the Home Office should be checking whether a pre-existing claim or right to citizenship exists before considering nationality applications. Where there is a possibility that an individual may already be British.

R (Roehrig) v Secretary of State for the Home Department[57]

In **Roehrig v SSHD** the Court accepted the Secretary of State's argument that children born between 1 January 1983 and 1 October 2000 to an EU national exercising their treaty rights are not automatic entitlement to British citizenship unless the EU parent had been granted Indefinite Leave to Remain at the time. As a result of the decision, the position for children born between 1 January 1983 and 1 October 2000 in those circumstances is that they would not be British automatically. The decision in **Roehrig** could also potentially impact their children, if they have had any.

57 [2023] EWHC 31 (Admin)

The Home Office has set out a number of steps to protect the British citizenship rights of those at risk following the decision, including updating the caseworker guidance to confirm that where someone has been previously recognised as a British citizen, such as acquiring a British passport, then that recognition should continue. As such if their British citizenship has been recognised, it would not be treated as a nullity. A Bill, the British Nationality (Regularisation of Past Practice) Bill, is currently making its way through Parliament to hopefully rectify the issue.

Nullity process

Where it is considered that the grant of citizenship is a nullity, a notice of intention to declare citizenship a nullity must be given by the Home Office to the person to whom it is intended to make such a declaration. The individual must be given an opportunity to respond to the allegations and to provide any information they wish to be taken into account by the Secretary of State. Individuals must be given 21 calendar days in which to respond.

Once the individual has responded, or if there is no response within 21 days, a decision on the case based on the information available will be made as to whether, on the facts of the case, the circumstances meet the Supreme Court nullity test. Once a decision has been made the individual must be notified if their grant of British citizenship has been declared a nullity. The decision must set out clearly how the individual's circumstances meet the Supreme Court test in **Hysaj**.

Consequences of nullity

Following the decision in **Hysaj**, the number of nullity decision taken by the Secretary of State have been significantly reduced. Grants of citizenship that previously would have been treated as null and void are now being considered under the deprivation provisions. The potential impact of delay by the Secretary of State in taking action under the deprivation provisions against an individual, because nullity was being contemplated was considered by the Upper Tribunal in respect of the appellant in **Hysaj**, when the Secretary of State decided to deprive him of his British citizenship; **Hysaj (Deprivation of Citizenship: Delay)**[58]**.**

An individual whose citizenship is declared null and void by the Secretary of State has no statutory right of appeal. Any challenge to the decision would therefore need to be made by way of an application for judicial review.

The nullity decision might render the individual liable to removal. The guidance the Secretary of State confirms that where an individual's citizenship has been declared null and void, they will normally revert to their previous immigration status. As such, provided the individual holds valid leave in an immigration category, that leave will continue as long as the Secretary of State remains satisfied that the criteria for granting such leave remains fulfilled. The guidance does however require consideration to be given to whether there are grounds to cancel the individual's permission to enter or stay under Part 9 of the Immigration Rules. Where an individual no longer has any status, a decision as to administrative removal or deportation would need to be taken.

The Secretary of State's decision to treat an individual's registration or naturalisation as a nullity can have unforeseen consequences for others, impacting on the position of their spouse or other relatives whose own immigration or citizenship status was secured on the basis of the nullified citizenship status.

---

[58] [2020] UKUT 128 (IAC)

Children

The guidance helpfully sets out the approach that the Secretary of State will take in different scenarios with regard to children born following their parent's registration/naturalisation as a British citizen, where that citizenship was later found to be a nullity:

i. Children who are born in the UK and whose parent was settled in the UK prior to becoming a citizen, may still be a British citizen. The nullity decision does not immediately alter previous leave.

ii. A child born overseas will not be a British citizen by descent, as their parent was not a British citizen at the time of the birth. The child would therefore not have the right of abode in the UK and would need to regularise their stay following the decision to treat their parent's citizenship as a nullity.

iii. Where a child registered as a British citizen at the same time as the parent registered or naturalised their registration may be a nullity. If the child registered as a British citizen in their true identity, then, notwithstanding that the grant to the parent is a nullity, the guidance states it would not be appropriate to take nullity action against the child. Where the child is registered under a false identity the SSHD may take action.

In all cases, when considering the impact of a nullity declaration on children the decision maker must remember to have due regard to the best interests of the child. As such any decision letter must demonstrate that all the information and evidence provided concerning the best interests of a relevant child has been considered. The guidance provides that documentary evidence from official or independent sources will be given more weight in the decision-making process than unsubstantiated assertions about a child's best interests. As such, those making representations should have regard to the quality of evidence being provided in support of cases and the potential impact on any children.

Spouses and partners

Where a foreign national has obtained permission to stay in the UK on the basis of being the spouse or partner of someone whose grant of British citizenship is a nullity the Home Office must consider if the permission of the foreign national spouse or partner should be cancelled. In cases where an individual has registered as a British citizen under section 6(2) of the British Nationality Act 1981 on the basis of being the spouse or partner of a British citizen, whose citizenship has been declared a nullity, the Home Office must consider if it is appropriate to deprive the spouse or partner on the grounds of fraud.

CHAPTER SIXTEEN

LOSS OF OTHER TYPES OF BRITISH NATIONALITY, RIGHT OF ABODE & PASSPORTS

Power to deprive

Section 40(1) of the BNA 1981 sets out that in addition to British citizens, the Secretary of State's powers of deprivation can be applied to those who are, British Overseas Territories citizens, British Overseas Citizens, British Nationals (Overseas), British Protected Persons or British subjects. Those powers can be exercised in the same way as for British citizens under s.40.

S.43 of BNA 1981, provides for the delegation of the power to deprive British Overseas Territories citizens of their nationality are to the Governor of each territory, with the Secretary of State's prior approval. Similarly, the Secretary of State can delegate the powers to the Lieutenant Governor of each of the 'the Islands' (Channel Islands and of the Isle of Man).

Nullity

The Secretary of State is also able to declare grants of other types of British nationality statuses including British Overseas Territories citizen, British Overseas Citizen, British National (Overseas), British Protected Person and British subject, a nullity. The same approach taken in respect of British citizenship will apply to the other types of British nationality. The remedy, judicial review, remains the same as well.

Deprivation of the 'right of abode'

Although not a type of nationality, some individuals have the right of abode in the UK even though they do not hold British nationality. However, the only way to acquire the right of abode since 1 Jan 1983 has been by becoming a British citizen.

The right of abode is defined in s.2 of the Immigration Act 1971 and in respect of those who are not British citizens applies under s.2(1)(b) to those who immediately before the commencement of the BNA 1981 were Commonwealth citizens with the right of abode and have continued to be Commonwealth citizens.

The requirement to have been continuously Commonwealth citizens means that those who are nationals of Pakistan, South Africa, The Gambia or the Republic of Maldives will not have the right of abode unless they are also British citizens due to their countries having left the Commonwealth at various points in time. Although Zimbabwe has withdrawn politically from the Commonwealth, it remains on the list of Commonwealth countries at Schedule 3 of the British Nationality Act 1981, and so its nationals can continue to have a right of abode in the UK as Commonwealth citizens provided, they had the right of abode immediately before the commencement of the Act.

The consequence of having the right of abode in the UK is that individuals are not subject to immigration control in the UK.

S.2A of the Immigration Act 1971 was inserted by s.57 of the Immigration, Asylum and Nationality Act 2006 (c. 13). It provides for the circumstances in which the Secretary of State may deprive an individual with the right of abode under s.2(1)(b) of the Immigration Act 1971 of that right. S.2A(2) provides that an order of deprivation may be made 'if the Secretary of State thinks it would be conducive to the public good for the person to be excluded or removed from the United Kingdom'.

A person against whom a deprivation order is made will have a right of appeal to Tribunal or, where sensitive information might otherwise be disclosed in the course of the appeal, to the Special Immigration Appeals Commission. Subject to the outcome of any such appeal, an order made under s.2A of the 1971 Act remains in force until revoked by the Secretary of State.

Deprivation of a British Passport

British citizens can also be refused a passport or have their passport withdrawn. Occasionally this will be the first step whilst an investigation into an individual's citizenship takes place. Applications for passports, for example where a request to vary personal details on them is made, often result in further enquiries being made and consideration of action to deprive an individual of their British citizenship, although not always.

British passports are issued at the discretion of the Secretary of Secretary for the Home Department under the Royal Prerogative. It is therefore done using an executive power which does not require legislation and as such a British national does not have a statutory right or an entitlement to a British passport. The same executive power can also be used by the Secretary of State to withdraw or withhold a passport from an individual.

Although sometimes the first step taken, the withdrawal or refusal to issue a passport is not the same as withdrawing citizenship. Someone whose passport is withdrawn remains a British citizen until such time as they are deprived of their citizenship or it is declared a nullity. Their ability to travel overseas will however be restricted, unless they hold a passport in a different nationality. If there are concerns that further action may be taken against the individual's British citizenship, caution should be exercised in leaving the country before the matter is resolved.

Home Office policy guidance states that a decision to withdraw a passport will be undertaken only "sparingly". An example given is where it is believed that an individual is intending to travel abroad in order to engage in terrorism.

There is no right of appeal against having a passport withdrawn or refused, an individual can however seek to have the decision reviewed by the Government or apply for a judicial review.

MORE BOOKS BY LAW BRIEF PUBLISHING

A selection of our other titles available now:-

'A Practical Guide to Estate Administration and Crypto Assets' by Richard Marshall
'A Practical Guide to Managing GDPR Data Subject Access Requests – Second Edition' by Patrick O'Kane
'A Practical Guide to Parental Alienation in Private and Public Law Children Cases' by Sam King QC & Frankie Shama
'Contested Heritage – Removing Art from Land and Historic Buildings' by Richard Harwood QC, Catherine Dobson, David Sawtell
'The Limits of Separate Legal Personality: When Those Running a Company Can Be Held Personally Liable for Losses Caused to Third Parties Outside of the Company' by Dr Mike Wilkinson
'A Practical Guide to Transgender Law' by Robin Moira White & Nicola Newbegin
'Artificial Intelligence – The Practical Legal Issues (2nd Edition)' by John Buyers
'A Practical Guide to Residential Freehold Conveyancing' by Lorraine Richardson
'A Practical Guide to Pensions on Divorce for Lawyers' by Bryan Scant
'A Practical Guide to Challenging Sham Marriage Allegations in Immigration Law' by Priya Solanki
'A Practical Guide to Legal Rights in Scotland' by Sarah-Jane Macdonald
'A Practical Guide to New Build Conveyancing' by Paul Sams & Rebecca East
'A Practical Guide to Defending Barristers in Disciplinary Cases' by Marc Beaumont
'A Practical Guide to Inherited Wealth on Divorce' by Hayley Trim
'A Practical Guide to Practice Direction 12J and Domestic Abuse in Private Law Children Proceedings' by Rebecca Cross & Malvika Jaganmohan
'A Practical Guide to Confiscation and Restraint' by Narita Bahra QC, John Carl Townsend, David Winch
'A Practical Guide to the Law of Forests in Scotland' by Philip Buchan
'A Practical Guide to Health and Medical Cases in Immigration Law' by Rebecca Chapman & Miranda Butler

'A Practical Guide to Bad Character Evidence for Criminal Practitioners by Aparna Rao
'A Practical Guide to Extradition Law post-Brexit' by Myles Grandison et al
'A Practical Guide to Hoarding and Mental Health for Housing Lawyers' by Rachel Coyle
'A Practical Guide to Psychiatric Claims in Personal Injury – 2nd Edition' by Liam Ryan
'Stephens on Contractual Indemnities' by Richard Stephens
'A Practical Guide to the EU Succession Regulation' by Richard Frimston
'A Practical Guide to Solicitor and Client Costs – 2nd Edition' by Robin Dunne
'Constructive Dismissal – Practice Pointers and Principles' by Benjimin Burgher
'A Practical Guide to Religion and Belief Discrimination Claims in the Workplace' by Kashif Ali
'A Practical Guide to the Law of Medical Treatment Decisions' by Ben Troke
'Fundamental Dishonesty and QOCS in Personal Injury Proceedings: Law and Practice' by Jake Rowley
'A Practical Guide to the Law in Relation to School Exclusions' by Charlotte Hadfield & Alice de Coverley
'A Practical Guide to Divorce for the Silver Separators' by Karin Walker
'The Right to be Forgotten – The Law and Practical Issues' by Melissa Stock
'A Practical Guide to Planning Law and Rights of Way in National Parks, the Broads and AONBs' by James Maurici QC, James Neill et al
'A Practical Guide to Election Law' by Tom Tabori
'A Practical Guide to the Law in Relation to Surrogacy' by Andrew Powell
'A Practical Guide to Claims Arising from Fatal Accidents – 2nd Edition' by James Patience
'A Practical Guide to the Ownership of Employee Inventions – From Entitlement to Compensation' by James Tumbridge & Ashley Roughton
'A Practical Guide to Asbestos Claims' by Jonathan Owen & Gareth McAloon
'A Practical Guide to Stamp Duty Land Tax in England and Northern Ireland' by Suzanne O'Hara
'A Practical Guide to the Law of Farming Partnerships' by Philip Whitcomb
'Covid-19, Homeworking and the Law – The Essential Guide to Employment and GDPR Issues' by Forbes Solicitors
'Covid-19 and Criminal Law – The Essential Guide' by Ramya Nagesh

'Covid-19 and Family Law in England and Wales – The Essential Guide' by Safda Mahmood
'A Practical Guide to the Law of Unlawful Eviction and Harassment – 2nd Edition' by Stephanie Lovegrove
'Covid-19, Brexit and the Law of Commercial Leases – The Essential Guide' by Mark Shelton
'A Practical Guide to Costs in Personal Injury Claims – 2nd Edition' by Matthew Hoe
'A Practical Guide to the General Data Protection Regulation (GDPR) – 2nd Edition' by Keith Markham
'Ellis on Credit Hire – Sixth Edition' by Aidan Ellis & Tim Kevan
'A Practical Guide to Working with Litigants in Person and McKenzie Friends in Family Cases' by Stuart Barlow
'Protecting Unregistered Brands: A Practical Guide to the Law of Passing Off' by Lorna Brazell
'A Practical Guide to Secondary Liability and Joint Enterprise Post-Jogee' by Joanne Cecil & James Mehigan
'A Practical Guide to the Pre-Action RTA Claims Protocol for Personal Injury Lawyers' by Antonia Ford
'A Practical Guide to Neighbour Disputes and the Law' by Alexander Walsh
'A Practical Guide to Forfeiture of Leases' by Mark Shelton
'A Practical Guide to Coercive Control for Legal Practitioners and Victims' by Rachel Horman
'A Practical Guide to Rights Over Airspace and Subsoil' by Daniel Gatty
'Tackling Disclosure in the Criminal Courts – A Practitioner's Guide' by Narita Bahra QC & Don Ramble
'A Practical Guide to the Law of Driverless Cars – Second Edition' by Alex Glassbrook, Emma Northey & Scarlett Milligan
'A Practical Guide to TOLATA Claims' by Greg Williams
'A Practical Guide to Elderly Law – 2nd Edition' by Justin Patten
'A Practical Guide to Responding to Housing Disrepair and Unfitness Claims' by Iain Wightwick
'A Practical Guide to the Construction and Rectification of Wills and Trust Instruments' by Edward Hewitt
'A Practical Guide to the Law of Bullying and Harassment in the Workplace' by Philip Hyland

'How to Be a Freelance Solicitor: A Practical Guide to the SRA-Regulated Freelance Solicitor Model' by Paul Bennett
'A Practical Guide to Prison Injury Claims' by Malcolm Johnson
'A Practical Guide to the Small Claims Track - 2nd Edition' by Dominic Bright
'A Practical Guide to Advising Clients at the Police Station' by Colin Stephen McKeown-Beaumont
'A Practical Guide to Antisocial Behaviour Injunctions' by Iain Wightwick
'Practical Mediation: A Guide for Mediators, Advocates, Advisers, Lawyers, and Students in Civil, Commercial, Business, Property, Workplace, and Employment Cases' by Jonathan Dingle with John Sephton
'The Mini-Pupillage Workbook' by David Boyle
'A Practical Guide to Crofting Law' by Brian Inkster
'A Practical Guide to Spousal Maintenance' by Liz Cowell
'A Practical Guide to the Law of Domain Names and Cybersquatting' by Andrew Clemson
'A Practical Guide to the Law of Gender Pay Gap Reporting' by Harini Iyengar
'NHS Whistleblowing and the Law' by Joseph England
'Employment Law and the Gig Economy' by Nigel Mackay & Annie Powell
'A Practical Guide to Noise Induced Hearing Loss (NIHL) Claims' by Andrew Mckie, Ian Skeate, Gareth McAloon
'An Introduction to Beauty Negligence Claims – A Practical Guide for the Personal Injury Practitioner' by Greg Almond
'Intercompany Agreements for Transfer Pricing Compliance' by Paul Sutton
'Zen and the Art of Mediation' by Martin Plowman
'A Practical Guide to the SRA Principles, Individual and Law Firm Codes of Conduct 2019 – What Every Law Firm Needs to Know' by Paul Bennett
'A Practical Guide to Adoption for Family Lawyers' by Graham Pegg
'A Practical Guide to Industrial Disease Claims' by Andrew Mckie & Ian Skeate
'A Practical Guide to Redundancy' by Philip Hyland
'A Practical Guide to Vicarious Liability' by Mariel Irvine
'A Practical Guide to Applications for Landlord's Consent and Variation of Leases' by Mark Shelton
'A Practical Guide to Relief from Sanctions Post-Mitchell and Denton' by Peter Causton

'A Practical Guide to Equity Release for Advisors' by Paul Sams
'A Practical Guide to Financial Services Claims' by Chris Hegarty
'The Law of Houses in Multiple Occupation: A Practical Guide to HMO Proceedings' by Julian Hunt
'Occupiers, Highways and Defective Premises Claims: A Practical Guide Post-Jackson – 2nd Edition' by Andrew Mckie
'A Practical Guide to Financial Ombudsman Service Claims' by Adam Temple & Robert Scrivenor
'A Practical Guide to Advising Schools on Employment Law' by Jonathan Holden
'A Practical Guide to Running Housing Disrepair and Cavity Wall Claims: 2nd Edition' by Andrew Mckie & Ian Skeate
'A Practical Guide to Holiday Sickness Claims – 2nd Edition' by Andrew Mckie & Ian Skeate
'Arguments and Tactics for Personal Injury and Clinical Negligence Claims' by Dorian Williams
'A Practical Guide to Drone Law' by Rufus Ballaster, Andrew Firman, Eleanor Clot
'A Practical Guide to Compliance for Personal Injury Firms Working With Claims Management Companies' by Paul Bennett
'RTA Allegations of Fraud in a Post-Jackson Era: The Handbook – 2nd Edition' by Andrew Mckie
'RTA Personal Injury Claims: A Practical Guide Post-Jackson' by Andrew Mckie
'On Experts: CPR35 for Lawyers and Experts' by David Boyle
'An Introduction to Personal Injury Law' by David Boyle

www.ingramcontent.com/pod-product-compliance
Lightning Source LLC
LaVergne TN
LVHW022106200926
848481LV00003B/1069
9781913715069